Implementation
Research

Also of interest from the Urban Institute Press:

The Digest of Social Experiments, Third Edition, by David Greenberg and Mark Shroder

Policy into Action: Implementation Research and Welfare Reform, edited by Mary Clare Lennon and Thomas Corbett

Social Experimentation and Policymaking, edited by David Greenberg, Donna Linksz, and Marvin Mandell

Welfare Reform: The Next Act, edited by Alan Weil and Kenneth Finegold

A Guide to
Implementation Research

ALAN WERNER

THE URBAN INSTITUTE PRESS
Washington, D.C.

THE URBAN INSTITUTE PRESS
2100 M Street, N.W.
Washington, D.C. 20037

Library of Congress Cataloging in Publication Data

Werner, Alan.
   A guide to implementation research / Alan Werner.
        p. cm.
   Includes bibliographical references (p. 147) and index.
   ISBN 0-87766-724-1 (pbk. : alk. paper)
   1. Evaluation research (Social action programs) 2. Public welfare—Evaluation.   I. Title.
   H62.W427 2004
   361.3'072—dc22

                                                            2004019247

Printed in the United States of America
10 09 08 07 06 05 04   1 2 3 4 5

THE URBAN INSTITUTE is a nonprofit policy research and educational organization established in Washington, D.C., in 1968. Its staff investigates the social, economic, and governance problems confronting the nation and evaluates the public and private means to alleviate them. The Institute disseminates its research findings through publications, its web site, the media, seminars, and forums.

Through work that ranges from broad conceptual studies to administrative and technical assistance, Institute researchers contribute to the stock of knowledge available to guide decisionmaking in the public interest.

Conclusions or opinions expressed in Institute publications are those of the authors and do not necessarily reflect the views of officers or trustees of the Institute, advisory groups, or any organizations that provide financial support to the Institute.

Contents

Preface ix

1 Introduction to Implementation Research 1

2 Data Needs, Sources, and Collection Strategies 27

3 Documenting Implementation 81

4 Assessing and Explaining Implementation 119

References 147

About the Author 151

Index 153

Preface

Guide to Implementation Research was conceived initially as a companion volume to the collection of articles included in *Policy into Action* (Lennon and Corbett 2003). The two books were to complement each other, with the guidebook intended as a more practical expression of the points and perspectives raised in the earlier volume of articles. However, each work stands on its own. Both books arose out of a series of conferences organized by Tom Corbett of the University of Wisconsin's Institute for Research on Poverty (IRP) and Barbara Blum of Columbia University's Research Forum on Children, Families, and the New Federalism at the National Center for Children. Beginning in 1996, the conferences brought together practitioners of implementation research from universities and research consulting firms, as well as consumers of evaluation research from state welfare agencies.

The focus of the conferences was to learn about recent research efforts to describe and evaluate the progress made by states and localities in implementing national welfare reform, but their larger purpose was to consolidate advances made in implementation research on social programs. With support from the Office of the Assistant Secretary for Planning and Evaluation of the U.S. Department of Health and Human Services and from the Joyce Foundation, several of the conference participants were commissioned to write articles that explore approaches to implementation research and their theoretical bases and assess their usefulness to policymakers and program practitioners. These articles were organized and published in *Policy into Action.*

The organizers of the implementation conferences asked me to develop a practical guidebook for students and researchers engaged in implementation research, as well as for consumers of implementation research. This book is the result.

A Guide to Implementation Research draws on the articles in *Policy into Action,* as well as on recent policy research and program evaluation. Because it arose out of the conferences and because of my research background, the book focuses on issues in the design and implementation of welfare reform policies and programs to illustrate specific research techniques and strategies. Those techniques and strategies, however, have broader application to research on a range of social programs. To assist readers less familiar with the context of welfare policy and welfare reform, chapter 1 includes a brief introduction to the challenges of designing and implementing welfare reform in the current policy context.

I would like to add a final note about theory. Although the book discusses several theories underlying specific approaches to implementation research, it does not itself rest on a particular theory. This decision is less a judgment about the usefulness of theory in informing implementation research as it is a resolution to allow the broadest possible application of the strategies and techniques presented. As such, the book is organized around what I find to be the core questions for implementation research: "What is happening?" "Is it what is expected or desired?" and "Why is it happening as it is?"

Alan Werner
Cambridge, Massachusetts

1

Introduction to
Implementation Research

Public policymakers and program managers are responsible for effectively and efficiently using community resources to promote social goals. Evaluation research provides information to support the decisions they make. This book explores how one type of evaluation research—implementation research—can assist those designing and operating social programs.

What Is Implementation Research?

In this book, "implementation research" is used as a general term for research that focuses on the question "What is happening?" in the design, implementation, administration, operation, services, and outcomes of social programs.[1] In the field of evaluation research, implementation studies are sometimes contrasted with impact studies, which measure the difference between "what is happening" and "what would have happened" in the program's absence. But although implementation studies do not estimate the impacts programs have on clients and other stakeholders, they do more than simply describe program experiences—implementation studies also assess and explain. That is, they not only ask, "What is happening?" but also "Is it what is expected or desired?" and "Why is it happening as it is?"

1

Comprehensive evaluations of social programs often include both implementation and impact studies. Within this research context, implementation studies can have multiple purposes, such as supporting the impact study by describing the precise nature of the program being tested and explaining the pattern of impact findings over time or across program sites.

Evaluations that include both impact and implementation studies are usually undertaken when policymakers, program administrators, and policy experts are uncertain about whether a given program or policy innovation will work. Often, however, new programs or policies are implemented on the basis of executive or legislative mandates, which may reflect some combination of changing public attitudes or values and knowledge already established through prior practice and research. These mandates oblige federal, state, and local agency executives and program managers to implement new programs or to make changes in existing programs. Particularly when the mandated changes are extensive and/or lead to the creation of new programs, the biggest concerns may be to get the programs "up and running" and working well. In these instances in particular, implementation research separate from an impact study may be warranted and desirable.

The core mission of implementation research to describe, assess, and explain "what is happening and why" may be especially compelling when brought to bear on the following major issues of program design, resources, administration, services, and outcomes:

What are the program goals, concept, and design? Are they based on sound theory and practice, and, if not, in what respects?
Social programs mandated by Congress, but implemented at the state or local level, are often launched with a block grant to states or communities, open-ended funding for an entitlement, or guaranteed federal matching funds, and are accompanied by rules about the use of those funds (such as eligibility, benefits, services) and a set of specific and general social goals. Within this framework, details of program design are often left to state and local officials. Sometimes implementation research may be concerned with fundamental questions of the soundness of program concept and design. For example, do the proposed services match the needs of the target population and are they likely to contribute to the program's goals? Are the planned administration and information systems feasible and suited to the desired "client flow" and management

information needs? In general, questions about theories behind program design help establish that the connections among program activities, systems, services, and client outcomes have some basis in research and experience, and that those activities, systems, and services are feasible given current technology and techniques.

Does the responsible agency (or agencies) have the resources and capacity available and in place to implement the program as planned, and if not, what is needed?

After considering a program's theoretical and practical feasibility, a logical next step is to assess the responsible agency's resources and capacity to implement the program and sustain its operation at a desired level. Implementation research may be designed to include the following questions about a program's resources and capacity: Has the program model been translated into concrete resource requirements? Is program funding sufficient to meet those requirements? Are the right staffing numbers and skills available among the agency's workforce or within the community? Can facilities handle client processing in the numbers and at the rate required? Are the necessary services available in adequate supply throughout the system? Can the current administrative and information systems accommodate the new program, and, if not, what more is required?

New programs rarely have the luxury of satisfying all capacity requirements before getting started. Agency managers usually expect to have to build up to capacity during the first months or years of a new program's life. Also, questions of program resources and capacity may arise at any time in the life of a program, and may be an important reason why program goals are not achieved. For example, as new policies add worker activities to ongoing responsibilities, capacity needs may outgrow available resources and some important tasks may not be accomplished. Even implementation studies of mature programs may thus face resource and capacity questions.

For example, even if issues of program capacity are settled enough for the program to operate at an acceptable level, a basic implementation challenge encompasses having the required facilities, administrative structures, information systems, and services in the right place at the right time. Offices may need to be rearranged to accommodate new procedures or to include space for mandatory meetings with clients. Similarly, new case management responsibilities may require a personal computer on every caseworker's desk. Moreover, administrative systems may require additional programming or new subsystems to meet the program's information needs. Finally, services envisioned in the program design must be arranged in advance to accommodate the expected streams of referred or assigned clients. An important part of most implementation studies is to describe and assess the degree to which the various components of a program appear to be ready and available to agency managers, workers, and clients, and, if not, to diagnose the reasons why.

Is the program suited to its environment?

Social programs do not exist in a vacuum. To be successful, they may require a receptive and well-informed client and advocacy community, as well as favorable social, political, and economic conditions. Program design should take the program's context into account, and may have to adjust to local differences in the environment by allowing for some amount of discretion or program variation across different communities. Implementation research often describes a program's environment and assesses the relationship between this environment and the program's operations and outcomes. For example, an implementation study may ask if a particular training program is preparing clients for jobs in accessible locations or if the program services and client behavioral requirements are suited to the beliefs and practices of major local ethnic groups.

Are program processes and systems operating as planned, and, if not, how and why?

Although a program may have adequate resources and may appear to have all of its components in place, it still may not operate as planned.[2] For example, if workers do not implement new policies and procedures, if new administrative systems do not work correctly, or if new communications links with service providers are not used, it is unlikely that the program will achieve its goals. Sometimes challenges related to changing institutional cultures are as important as these operational and structural issues. For example, are workers internalizing new goals and policies and effectively communicating them to clients? Are quality assurance and performance monitoring systems in place to reinforce the program's change in direction? Typically, implementation researchers will observe program operations, measure the degree to which they are operating as planned, diagnose problems, and recommend solutions.

Is the program reaching the intended target population with the appropriate services, at the planned rate and "dosage," and, if not, how and why?
Although the quality and quantity of a program's services may be thought of as part of its operations, it is sometimes convenient to focus on services separately. This is particularly true if service delivery is decentralized and/or other agencies or businesses provide the services. If critical program services are not provided in sufficient numbers in a reasonable time, or if services are inappropriate or of low quality, overall program goals may not be met. To address these issues, implementation studies often observe, measure, and assess service provision, as well as diagnose observed problems and recommend changes.

Are clients achieving desired outcomes, and, if not, how and why?[3]
Although client outcomes are the result of all the program aspects discussed above, outcomes are often the first signs that a program may or may not be working well. Sometimes, dissatisfaction with results may also prompt program managers, state executives, or the state legislature to undertake an implementation study in the first place.[4] In uncovering the reasons why a program is unsuccessful in achieving results, implementation research may call into question any or all of the parts of a program, including, for example, the program's design and theoretical underpinnings, relationship to its environment, administrative and management structure, resources, policies and procedures, and services.

What Research Methods Are Included in Implementation Studies?

While some researchers think of implementation research as a specific methodology, this book defines implementation research as the set of specific issues that fall within the core questions, "What is happening?" "Is it what is expected or desired?" and "Why is it happening as it is?" When characterized by the pursuit of these questions, implementation research is eclectic and pragmatic in its methodologies—the data, data collection strategies, analyses, and presentational styles required are determined by a combination of its specific research questions and an educated guess by the researchers about where and how to look for the answers.[5] The following section introduces and summarizes the variety of data and analyses that may be included in implementation research; later chapters describe and illustrate them in greater detail.

Data and Data Collection

Because implementation studies may address almost any phenomena related to the way a social program operates, they can encompass a wide variety of data and data collection strategies. This section introduces the types of data usually collected for implementation research.

Many of the primary data needed for implementation research are gathered firsthand in the "field" or where program activities happen and client outcomes are realized. A large portion of needed data are firsthand accounts of program processes, experiences, opinions, and results by the key stakeholders, including program planners and developers, state agency managers, local office management and staff, service provider management and staff, state and local advocacy and public interest groups, and clients. Researchers use a variety of methods to gather information on site from these respondents, including the following examples:

- *Open-ended interviews.* These are semistructured conversations that focus on those parts of the program or program experiences most relevant to the informant being interviewed.
- *Focus groups.* Focus groups are open-ended discussion groups, usually of no more than 10 to 15 people of similar backgrounds, organized around some small set of topics or themes.
- *Participant observation.* Participant observation is a specialized tool of ethnographic research that places the researcher for extended periods of time in a program's social milieu in an attempt to understand the program from the clients' viewpoint.

Some implementation questions require information on relatively large numbers of people, such as questions that ask about the "average" client or the "average" caseworker, or those that ask about how some client groups or local areas are different from other groups or communities. Generally, there are two types of data that include individual information ("microdata") about large numbers of people: administrative data and survey data. Administrative data are routinely collected as part of program operations, and may include both electronic and hard-copy case files. Automated administrative data are usually quantitative or categorical (such as gender or ethnicity), but hard-copy administrative data may also include case note narratives and other qualitative information.

Surveys involve collecting data from large numbers of respondents. The usual modes for surveys are mail, telephone, and in-person interviews; sometimes surveys use a combination of these approaches. Researchers design survey questionnaires so that collected information or responses may be easily converted into quantitative measures, but also may include open-ended or qualitative responses.

Administrative data are also often available in statistical reports that may be important sources of information about program operations, activities, and outcomes. The federal government or state legislatures sometimes require state agencies to issue statistical reports that monitor program performance and program spending. Other statistical reports may be useful in understanding a program's environment, such as U.S. Census or state vital statistics reports. Other useful statistical reports are compiled by business groups or by other public and special interest groups. Many public agencies have developed web sites that often have statistical summaries of agency activities and accomplishments.

Agency documents related to program planning, design, start-up, administration, and public information are a final source of data for implementation research. These documents may include relevant federal and state legislation and administrative rules, mandated federal and state program plans and documents supporting the plans, implementation plans, worker manuals and handbooks, program forms, press kits, and newspaper articles.

Documenting, Assessing, and Explaining Implementation

Implementation research has a variety of analytic strategies at its disposal, depending on the data used and the goal of the analysis—documenting ("What is happening?"), assessing ("Is it what we want or expect to happen?"), and explaining ("Why is it happening as it is?") program implementation. Why are assessment and explanation treated separately in this book? After all, within the context of an impact study, assessment and explanation are nearly the same. That is, impact studies are designed to assess the degree to which a program or policy is causing desired change. In social science, demonstrating that b is caused by a usually means that b is explained by a.

In implementation research, however, "assessment" and "explanation" mean different things. "Assessment" means judging whether or not the program or policy under study is operating according to some model, norm, or standard. "Explanation" means generating hypotheses about why the policy or program is operating as it is and achieving its results. Implementation research is usually not expected to test those causal hypotheses.[6]

The following is an overview of the types of analyses used in implementation research; chapters 3 and 4 present more detailed accounts of how these strategies may be used to address specific research questions.

Documenting Implementation

Documenting how a program operates is at the core of implementation research. Certainly, it is difficult to understand whether a program is operating as planned and is achieving its intended goals, or why a program is operating as it is, without a clear picture of what is happening in the program. There are two fundamental perspectives implementation research may adopt when describing a social program. First, and most often, the story is told from the point of view of the objective researcher. Although the objective description may include accounts of stakeholder opinions and attitudes, it presents them as important "facts" about the program rather than as alternative or competing descriptions of the program. Sometimes, however, it is also important to describe the program from the point of view of the program's stakeholders. In trying to understand why a program operates as it does, this insider's view can often clarify the program actors' motivations, knowledge, and attitudes, thus helping explain their interactions with the program and providing insight into "what is *really* happening" in program administration.

Researchers designing and conducting a study to document implementation face several major challenges:

- Developing an initial idea of what to observe, whom to interview, and what to ask;
- Sorting through conflicting or even contradictory descriptions and assessments of a program;
- Dealing with variations over time and across program sites; and
- Combining quantitative and qualitative data in cogent and useful ways.

Assessing Implementation

Implementation studies provide assessments of program designs, operations, and outcomes. In general, implementation assessments consist of comparing data on program operations, activities, services, and outcomes with some norm or standard and developing an evaluation based on that comparison. In conducting assessments, researchers may appeal to numerous norms or standards, depending on the activity, structure, or outcome evaluated, including the following examples:

- The initial program model, plan, or design;
- Federal and state legislative or administrative rules and performance standards;
- Professional or industry standards;
- Implementation researchers' professional experience and judgment; and
- Opinions and judgments of the program's stakeholders.

Explaining Implementation

Through explanatory analysis, implementation research seeks to understand why a program operates and performs as it does, as well as develop recommendations for change or lessons for effective program design and administration. The issue of whether implementation research alone can establish causal links between program policies, program activities, client outcomes, and broader social change is an ongoing controversy. This book does not engage in the debate, but takes the position that while well-designed implementation research can uncover *plausible* reasons why a program is working or not—can build hypotheses and theories—it should not be expected to demonstrate causality conclusively (see endnotes 3 and 6).

Most explanatory analysis in implementation research uses one or more of three general approaches in developing hypotheses about causal connections: (1) using stakeholder accounts of why they take, or fail to take, specific actions related to program activities and goals; (2) associating natural or planned variations in management, policies, operations, services, or other factors with observed differences in results; and (3) monitoring results against predictions or expectations based on the program's model or theory.

Advantages and Limitations of Implementation Research

As with any research approach, implementation research has both advantages and limitations when compared with alternative methodologies. As mentioned above, implementation research conducted in conjunction with an impact evaluation provides detailed information "inside the black box"—information about how programs operate and how impacts happen. However, stand-alone implementation studies also have important advantages and limitations as compared with impact studies. Among the advantages of implementation research are the following:

- *Provides rapid feedback to program managers.* When necessary, implementation studies can be designed and fielded quickly. Because the study of "what is happening" and program operations can occur concurrently, implementation research can feed timely information back to managers and policymakers. In contrast, impact studies often require several years of follow-up to track changes caused by the program.
- *Provides information during a program's formative period.* Sometimes the need for information about operations and results is greatest during the program's formative period. Impact studies are most useful when they evaluate mature, stable programs, but implementation studies may be mounted at any time. In fact, stand-alone implementation studies are often used to monitor and fine-tune operations during a program's start-up phase. A related advantage of implementation studies is that they can take place during periods of rapid and widespread program and contextual change and in an environment of uncertainty about how and when the program will stabilize and what its final structure will be.
- *Provides rich contextual and ethnographic information.* Implementation studies can enhance policymakers' and program managers' knowledge of the various environments in which programs operate and their knowledge of how workers and clients experience the program. This information may be important for programs whose success depends in part on changing the "culture" of the program, worker-client communication and interaction, and stakeholders' attitudes about the program and its goals. Moreover, by collecting data from a variety of stakeholders, implementation research typically includes multiple perspectives on key program and policy issues.

- *Provides information about the program "as it really is."* One prevailing type of impact study—experimental design—depends on randomly assigning people potentially affected by the program into two groups: one that receives the program intervention and one that does not. Some researchers have noted that imposing random assignment on an ongoing program can alter operations and introduce unwanted "noise" into the evaluation. However, implementation studies alter the normal course of operations very little, if at all.

- *Provides limited and strategic information where and when necessary.* A final important advantage of implementation research over longer-term impact studies is that implementation studies can be targeted and strategic. That is, researchers can design implementation studies efficiently to look only at one aspect of operations or to focus on a particular locality or program office. In contrast, impact studies usually require a sizable investment of resources, as large samples of program clients often need to be followed up over a long period of time.

Among the important limitations of implementation research are the following:

- *Does not provide direct and accurate estimates of program impacts or cost-effectiveness.* Because implementation studies are not designed to estimate impacts, they will not provide accurate estimates of program impacts or, by extension, estimates of program cost-effectiveness (cost per unit of "impact") or cost-benefit ratios. Implementation studies are not substitutes for well-designed impact studies.

- *Makes some judgments on the basis of qualitative and/or subjective data.* As suggested above, some of the data collected for implementation research are quantitative in nature. Analyses using those data are subject to the same standards of statistical rigor as quantitative data used for impact evaluations. Some judgments needed for implementation evaluations, however, must be made on the basis of qualitative or subjective data. For example, assessments about changes in the "culture of a bureaucracy" may be based on a combination of observer judgment and respondent opinion, with few "hard" statistical data to back the assessment up. Some researchers consider the reliance on qualitative and subjective data to be a drawback to implementation research. Nevertheless, those judgments are often of value to program managers and can be a critical dimension to program evaluation when considered with other indicators of operations and results.

How This Book Is Organized

Implementation research may be applied to evaluation research across the spectrum of social policies and programs. The purpose of this book is to provide practical guidance to consumers and practitioners in applying implementation research to evaluation studies in all types of social policies and programs. Because this book grew out of efforts to develop standards for implementation research for welfare reform programs, and because of my background and experience in welfare policy and programs, most of the examples in this book are taken from that policy domain.

Using the general framework introduced above, the next section of this chapter provides an overview of how to organize a comprehensive implementation study of a welfare reform program through specific research questions. The section also gives an introduction to the welfare reform movement of the 1990s so that the reader can understand the issues involved in designing and conducting implementation research for welfare reform.

This book is not intended to be exhaustive, but to suggest the range of research questions and techniques available to implementation studies and the results that may be expected. Moreover, it is not intended to argue for any one point of view or methodology, but to be representative of the range of approaches that have been effectively used. Toward that end, the book includes examples of implementation research of welfare reform programs by research consulting firms, academic practitioners, and government agencies.

The Challenges of Welfare Reform

The 1980s and 1990s witnessed growing popular demand for changes in American welfare policy. Trends in public opinion were paralleled by the accelerating pace of experimentation in welfare policies and programs, particularly at the state and local level. Growing confidence in more dynamic alternatives to need-based cash assistance programs that had been in force since the 1930s combined with political will in the passage of the Personal Responsibility and Work Opportunity Reconciliation Act (PRWORA) of 1996. There are three core elements of PRWORA:

- It converted open-ended federal support for cash assistance (Aid to Families with Dependent Children [AFDC]) into fixed block grants to states (Temporary Assistance for Needy Families [TANF]).
- It gave states unprecedented discretion in designing welfare policies, programs, and services; in spending block grant monies on related services for low-income families; and in transferring authority and responsibility for these decisions to more local political entities.
- It limited the use of federal TANF funds to families that have been receiving cash assistance for less than 60 months and imposed other fiscal penalties on states that do not meet various performance standards related to clients' participation in work, work preparation, and other key behaviors.

The implications of these three core elements for the design, operation, and assessment of welfare programs and related programs and services are enormous. Because states are now fiscally responsible for any monies spent on TANF benefits or services beyond the amount of the TANF block grant, as well as for individuals who have received TANF funds or services for more than 60 months in a lifetime, there is a strong incentive to limit welfare use and to move families quickly to economic independence. Those incentives for states to encourage work as an alternative to welfare are strengthened by the threat of fiscal penalties for failure to meet federal standards for the proportion of clients who work or prepare for work.

With the deep-seated changes in policy, goals, expectations, and philosophy coincident with recent welfare reform, welfare programs are undergoing a "paradigm shift" in their basic design.[7] That is, rather than a series of small and tightly controlled innovations made to a stable core policy and administrative structure, recent welfare reform looks more like the creation of a new program, with new goals, policies, services, administrative systems, and bureaucratic cultures emerging from state and federal mandates. In an environment in which so many aspects of welfare programs and services are shifting at once, it is likely premature to implement impact evaluations for at least two important reasons. First, because so many factors that may affect program outcomes are evolving at the same time, it would be difficult to isolate the impact of one or several policies or services, even with a classical experimental design. Second, it is difficult to predict in advance exactly what the "new system" will look like and how it will operate. This is exactly the situation in which a stand-alone implementation study may be called upon to address the questions "What is happening?" "Is it what we expected?" and "Why is it happening as it is?"

Designing an Implementation Study of a Welfare Reform Program: Research Questions

Unlike the textbook approach to scientific inquiry—framing, testing, and reframing the hypothesis—implementation research does not always begin with a hypothesis (although it may lead to hypotheses about how and why things work). Nevertheless, any coherent research project must be guided by some plan; investigators cannot simply "go out and look at the program." At the very least, researchers must know something about the program goals and design. Some idea of the design, prescribed policies and activities, and desired outcomes may then be used to guide the development of detailed questions about the program environment, operations, and results. The questions suggest what to look for (data), where and how to look (data collection), and how to use the information strategically (analysis plans).

The opening of this chapter showed how the questions that drive the organization of an implementation study may be related to the logic of the program model. In addition, the ways in which the program is structured and operated may help bring about a set of specific and general social goals. As mentioned previously, an implementation study need not address all aspects of a program to be useful. For example, an implementation study may focus on the delivery of services to clients, the organization and use of administrative information, or on clients' responses to program requirements and opportunities. To give some idea of the breadth of research activities that may go on in an implementation study, this book addresses the logical and practical steps in the design, development, and implementation of a welfare reform program. Using the categories introduced at the beginning of the chapter, the following section translates those general categories into specific research questions that may be part of an implementation study of a welfare program.

What are the program goals, concept, and design? Are they based on sound theory and practice, and, if not, in what respects?
This set of questions asks about the general and specific program goals and requirements, how the program is designed to help meet those goals, and the theoretical and practical connections between the program design and its goals. In addition to describing the program design and its underpinnings, researchers often are interested in understanding how the program was developed and why certain design choices were made. Although the process of program planning and development does not necessarily indicate whether the right choices were made, it allows some insight into the rationale behind those choices and the interests they represent. Questions of this type may include the following:

- How was the program planned and developed? Who were the principal actors and what were their views about the program's goals and design? What compromises, if any, were made during program planning and development? Were those compromises sensible in view of the final program design?
- What general and specific goals is the program designed to meet? Are the goals feasible on the basis of prior research and practice?
- What are the federal, state, and local legal and administrative requirements guiding allowable and/or preferred policies, procedures, activities, and services? Are those requirements compatible with the program's goals?
- How are the program's prescribed policies, procedures, activities, and services designed to advance the program's general and specific goals?
- What is the design of "client flow" through the program? What administrative systems are required to support program operations? Are they feasible?
- What are the levels and timing of activities, services, and client participation required to achieve the program's specific goals? Are they feasible on the basis of prior research and practice?
- What are the theoretical and practical bases connecting the program's design to its goals? Are they sound, and, if not, how and why? How may the program's design be improved to help achieve its goals?

What are the types and levels of resources needed to implement the program as planned?
This set of questions addresses the resource issues implied by the program's design and its goals for client outcomes. This part of an implementation study may be a critical first step in assessing the practical feasibility of a program's design and its likely success. Among the questions falling under this rubric are the following:

- What types of resources (e.g., physical plant, services, staffing number and expertise, and information systems) do the program's design and goals require? What levels of resources are needed to operate the program? What are the budgetary implications?
- What are the sources of the program's needed resources? For example, what parts of the program's activities and services will be operated by the welfare department, by other agencies, or contracted out to private providers? To what degree are these arrangements already in place and to what degree will they have to be developed? What experience does the welfare agency have in coordinating services with other agencies and institutions?
- Are the program's resource requirements likely to be met, given the program's budget, available resources, and resources to be developed? If not, how and why?

Is the program suited to its environment?
These questions address the relationship between the program and its demographic, social, cultural, political, and economic environment. Although sometimes treated as part of the investigation of a program's concept and design, the environment is also a critical dimension in understanding a program's operations and results. Among the questions arising out of this part of an implementation study are the following:

- What are the demographic, social, cultural, political, and economic environments in which the program will operate? How does the environment differ across the state?
- In what ways has the program's environment affected its implementation, operations, and results?
- In what ways have variations in the program's local environment led to variations in program design and operations? What implications do these variations have for the program's goals and results?

Are the resources to operate the program in place and, if not, how and why?
This set of questions refers to the resource requirements for program administration and operations and asks whether those requirements have been met. As discussed previously, a new program may require some time to "get up to scale," and the answers to these questions may vary depending on when they are asked. Nevertheless, it is appropriate to ask these questions at any stage of a program's life, as performance may be vitally dependent on the level of available resources. Some specific questions that may be included in this category are the following:

- Are all required resources available, including
  o Number, location, and infrastructure of local offices and/or other entry and contact points needed for the expected type and number of clientele.
  o Number and types of management and staff needed to maintain target caseloads and types and levels of service.
  o Number and types of activities and services planned to meet client needs and performance benchmarks, including services provided by other agencies and institutions.
  o Information systems needed for individual case management as well as for program management.
- Which resources are in short supply and why? How does this vary by locality?
- What implication does the level of resources have for operations and performance?

Are program processes and systems operating as planned, and, if not, how and why?
This group of research questions and the next form the basis for studies focused on program operations, or "process studies." The questions under this first group are concerned with the program operations. Although the distinction between questions about program operations and questions about scale and quality of services (the next group) is somewhat arbitrary, the two groups require different data collection and measurement techniques. The following are some examples of specific questions in this group:

- Is the application process working as planned, including, for example
  o Do applicants know where to go as they enter the office building or program area?

- ○ Are applicants connected with eligibility workers as planned?
- ○ Do eligibility workers follow new procedures and apply new policies when conducting eligibility interviews?
- ○ Do workers communicate new eligibility standards and requirements to applicants?
- ○ Do workers process applicant information correctly and on time?
- • Are workers implementing the new policies and procedures regarding behavioral requirements for applicants and recipients, including, for example
  - ○ Are workers making appointments with applicants and/or recipients for program orientations and/or assessments?
  - ○ Are applicants and recipients being referred to appropriate services and activities?
  - ○ Are workers performing prescribed applicant and recipient follow-up and monitoring?
- • Are ongoing eligibility and benefit policies being followed, including, for example
  - ○ Are workers performing eligibility determinations using new procedures and policies?
  - ○ Are workers collecting and acting on information about the financial and other eligibility status conditions of recipient families?
- • Are applicants and clients attending the various education, employment, training, work experience, workfare, and other referred activities and services? Are applicants and clients being provided with needed supportive services?
- • Are associated agencies and service providers delivering agreed-upon and contracted services according to program expectations and policies, as well as communicating client progress, outcomes, and failures to comply in an accurate and timely fashion to TANF program case managers?
- • Are information systems operating as planned, including containing required data fields and expected computational and presentational capabilities? Are the right people getting easy and timely access to needed data? Are workers updating data fields as expected? Is the information included in the administrative system being used as planned?
- • How and why are various program processes and systems not operating as planned? Does this vary by locality? What are the implica-

tions for program operations and performance and client outcomes? How may program processes and systems be improved?

Is the program reaching the intended target population with the appropriate services, at the planned rate and "dosage," and, if not, how and why? As mentioned above, this group of research questions is concerned with the quantity, quality, and timing of program activities and services, as opposed to questions of whether or not the right activities and services are happening at all. This part of an implementation study is particularly important when considering the likely connection between program activities and services, and client outcomes. That is, if the program is likely to have its intended impact on families, it must provide prescribed services to sufficient numbers of clients within the expected time frame. Some specific research questions addressing these issues include the following examples:

- How often are individual or group orientations scheduled? What proportion of clients scheduled for orientations actually attend those orientations? On average, how long do clients wait for a scheduled orientation? On average, how many attend orientations? What is the content and quality of the orientations?
- What is the attendance rate for individual and/or group employability assessments?
- What proportion of applicants and clients are expected to engage in work or a work-related activity? How many applicants and clients are engaging in work or a work-related activity? Are proper and timely compliance and sanctioning procedures being followed for applicants and clients who do not engage in work or a work-related activity? If not, how and why?
- What work or work-related activities or services are clients assigned to or choose to engage in? For each type of activity,
  - What number and proportion of clients are assigned?
  - What number and proportion begin the activity or service?
  - On average, how long do clients wait before beginning the activity or service?
  - On average, what number and proportion of clients are engaged in an activity or service in a given time period?
  - On average, how long do clients remain in the activity or service? Is this for a longer or shorter period than expected?

- On average, how many hours per week does the activity or service require? How many hours per week do clients spend on the activity or service?
- What is the content and quality of the activity or service? Is it sufficient to meet program expectations? If not, how and why?
- What supportive services are available to applicants and recipients? For each supportive service,
  - How many clients need or request the service?
  - How many receive or use the service?
  - Is the service available for all who need it? If not, why and how? On average, how long does someone have to wait for the service?
  - What is the content and quality of the supportive service? Is it sufficient to meet program expectations? If not, how and why?
- What are the implications of the content, timing, and quality of services for program operations and performance? How does this vary by locality? How may services be improved?

Is the program achieving desired outcomes, and, if not, how and why?
A final set of questions focuses on program results, at both the "micro" and "macro" level. At the micro level, implementation researchers want to know what happens to individual applicants and clients as they pass through the program and are subject to its policies, procedures, behavioral requirements, and services. At the macro level, studies focus on overall changes in the administrative and institutional culture of welfare and whether the reform effort has substantially changed worker, client, and the public's attitudes and expectations about welfare. Some important questions about program outcomes include the following examples:

- How many clients become employed, and in what time frame? What types of jobs in what industries are clients finding? What are the characteristics of clients' jobs, including, for example, wages, hours, and benefits? What is the record of job retention?
- How many families are achieving financial independence (leaving welfare), in what time frame, and for what reasons?
- What are the changes in families' sources of income and total income?
- What are the changes in families' household and living arrangements?
- What are the changes in children's well-being?
- How and why do the above vary by locality? By demographic or other characteristics?

- To what degree have client and worker expectations as well as the "culture of welfare" changed?
- Is the program achieving its goals for client and other outcomes? If not, how and why? How may program performance be improved?

The Flexibility of the Implementation Research Agenda

This long list of research questions that guide implementation research is based on a provisional understanding of what the program is trying to do and how it is trying to do it. Beginning with specific questions helps the researcher identify the study's quarry—the data and data sources needed to answer the general questions: "What is happening?" "Is it what we expected?" and "Why is it happening as it is?" One great advantage of implementation research, however, is its flexibility. Because the study is not locked into testing a set of hypotheses specified beforehand, it can shift its focus as it gathers data and fleshes out the program's details. Some preliminary research questions may become moot and new questions may arise. Particularly in studies of new programs or of widespread changes in existing programs, researchers must be prepared to change their focus or adopt new lines of questioning as the program's actual shape emerges.

One example of the need to be flexible in an implementation research study is offered by an evaluation of a welfare reform demonstration in New York State tested in the 1980s—the Comprehensive Employment Opportunity Support Center (CEOSC) program (see Werner and Nutt-Powell 1988). CEOSC was an intensive education, employment, and training program for longer-term welfare clients with preschool children. The program was operated either by special units of a county's welfare department or by private not-for-profit social service agencies. Part of the rationale for this approach was to set CEOSC off from "business as usual" in the welfare department's regular income maintenance units.

Initially, the evaluation research plan focused on the administrative structure, activities, and services of the CEOSC program site or unit. The first site visits to CEOSC programs made it clear that participants' relationship with their eligibility workers was a critical dimension of program success. First, CEOSC participants relied on eligibility workers for reimbursements for transportation, childcare, and other training expenses. Second, and more subtly, the eligibility workers' acceptance of

CEOSC was an important element in building participants' confidence in volunteering for, and remaining involved in, CEOSC. The inherent flexibility of a stand-alone implementation study allowed the researchers to add, change, or remove critical research questions as the study progressed.

Getting Started

Each succeeding chapter in this guidebook builds upon the previous chapters in developing a blueprint for an implementation study of welfare reform, although the approaches discussed are applicable to a wide range of programs. Table 1.1 includes some illustrative research questions and the type of inquiry each represents (i.e., documenting ["What is happening?"], assessing ["Is it what is expected or desired?"], or explaining ["Why is it happening?"]).

Table 1.1. *Implementation Study Research Questions*

Implementation research domain and illustrative questions	Type of question
Theoretical and practical basis	
How was the program planned and developed?	Documenting
What goals is the program designed to meet? Are they feasible?	Documenting Assessing
How are the program's prescribed policies, procedures, activities, and services designed to advance the program's general and specific goals?	Documenting Assessing
What is the design of "client flow" and the administrative systems? Is it feasible?	Documenting Assessing
What are the theoretical and practical bases connecting the program's design to its goals? Are they sound, and, if not, how and why? How may the program's design be improved to help achieve its goals?	Documenting Explaining
Resource requirements and capacity	
What types of resources are required?	Documenting
What are the sources of the program's needed resources?	Documenting
Are the program's resource requirements likely to be met, given the program's budget, available resources, and resources to be developed? If not, how and why?	Assessing Explaining

(continued)

Table 1.1. *Continued*

Implementation research domain and illustrative questions	Type of question
Program environment	
What are the demographic, social, cultural, political, and economic environments in which the program operates?	Documenting
In what ways has the program's environment affected its implementation, operations, and results?	Explaining
In what ways have variations in the program's local environment led to variations in program design and operations? What implications do these variations have for the program's goals and results?	Documenting Explaining
Are the necessary resources to operate the program "in place"?	
Are all required resources available?	Documenting
Which resources are in short supply and why? How does this vary by locality?	Documenting
What implications does the level of resources have for program operations and performance?	Explaining
Are program processes and systems operating as planned?	
Are all program processes and systems operating as planned?	Documenting Assessing
How and why are various program processes and systems not operating as planned? Does this vary by locality? What are the implications for program performance and client outcomes? How may program processes and systems be improved?	Assessing Explaining
Is the program reaching the intended target population with the intended services?	
How many clients are scheduled for various program activities and services? What proportion of clients scheduled for program activities and services attend as scheduled? What other services are clients using?	Documenting
What are the content and quality of program activities or services? Are the content and quality sufficient to meet program expectations? If not, how and why?	Documenting Assessing
What are the implications of the content, timing, and quality of services for program operations and performance? How does this vary by locality? How may services be improved?	Explaining
Is the program achieving desired outcomes?	
What are the relevant outcomes of program clients? What are the changes in their overall well-being?	Documenting
To what degree have client and worker expectations as well as the "culture of welfare" changed?	Documenting
Is the program achieving its goals for client and other outcomes? If not, how and why? How may program performance be improved?	Assessing Explaining

NOTES

1. Occasionally, "implementation research" is used in the narrower sense of studies of the design, planning, and especially the initial operating phase, or start up, of a program. Sometimes, "implementation research" and "process research" are used synonymously, but "process research" is also used in a more limited way to refer to the study of a program's internal operations and relationships.

2. Note that an implementation study may be warranted even if programs are operating as planned. For example, well-operating programs may be improved or may deserve study because they can provide guidance to other agency operations or to similar programs elsewhere. Note also that a program may not be working as planned but may still produce its intended outcomes (and/or other beneficial outcomes). In these instances, implementation research may help shed light on how the program is working and whether it represents a better alternative to the initial program model.

3. Note that this question avoids phrasing that implies a program is "producing" or "causing" changes in outcomes (such as increasing employment among welfare recipients). This is in keeping with our definition of implementation research that includes "outcomes" but not "impacts." For example, it is legitimate to ask an implementation study to address the following question: "Do participants in the program's adult literacy class have higher reading scores after taking the class, and, if not, what are some possible explanations why?" On the other hand, it would take an impact study to answer the following question: "To what degree are the reading scores of participants in the program's adult literacy class higher than they would have been in the absence of the class or with some alternative treatment?"

Sometimes the distinction between outcomes and impacts results in the mistaken impression that implementation studies must never deal with issues of *causality*. Implementation studies are usually limited to describing outcomes without being able to estimate how much (if any) of a change in client outcomes was caused by the program intervention. However, implementation studies also attempt to *explain* observed outcomes. That is, implementation studies investigate assumed causal connections between program services and client outcomes. For example, the design of an implementation study and its research focus is based on some notion—whether implicitly or explicitly—of how the parts of a program interrelate and how the program is supposed to change client outcomes. Except in the rare instances in which *only* the intervention and no other factor could possibly have affected given outcomes, however, an implementation study is not designed to estimate the degree to which observed changes are due to the intervention. Rather, an implementation study can only indicate that the program *may* or *may not* be changing client behavior and outcomes as predicted by the ideas underlying the program design. Implementation studies may also generate new hypotheses about alternative potential causal processes at work. But only a well-designed impact study can indicate, within established standards of statistical precision, whether an intervention *is* or *is not* having an impact on client behavior and outcomes.

4. Questions about a program's effectiveness in realizing its goals may not be the only reason to engage in implementation research. For example, even if a program appears to be working well, it may be important for implementation research to ask

"How can the program be made more effective?" Similarly, if a program seems to be achieving exemplary results, another important implementation study question may be "Why does this program work so well and can it be replicated elsewhere?"

5. This is not to say that theory has no place in implementation research. Some approaches to implementation research are based on theories about how social programs operate (see chapter 4).

6. An important exception is "administrative modeling," discussed in more detail with examples in chapter 4. This approach uses statistical techniques that may, under the right conditions, indicate causal connections between given aspects of a program's organization or operations and program results. The important thing to note about this type of analysis is that it is not expected to allow policymakers to choose *among* alternative program or policy environments (as in a well-designed impact study), but rather to help policymakers and program managers make better administrative and operational choices *within* a given program and policy environment. See Mead (2003).

7. For the concept of a "paradigm shift," see Kuhn (1962) and Corbett (1997).

2

Data Needs, Sources, and Collection Strategies

I n the preceding chapter, general areas of research—such as the theo-retical and practical basis for the program, the resource requirements, and whether the program is reaching its intended participants—helped formulate specific questions relevant to welfare reform programs. Part of the purpose of developing a list of detailed questions from an imple-mentation study's overall research goals is to help clarify information needs. This chapter surveys the various data sources and data collection techniques used by implementation researchers to meet those informa-tion requirements. The chapter is organized into three major sections: planning data collection, conducting interviews and observations on site, and other data collection activities.

Planning Data Collection

Data Needs and Sources

The broad range of research questions implementation research addresses calls for an equally wide variety of data. For example, questions about planning and development usually lead to written and oral accounts of the planning process, as well as to documentation of the various stages of pro-gram design and the debates and decisions that led to the final program model. On the other hand, descriptions and evaluations of operations usually require some combination of quantitative data documenting participation patterns and client characteristics with qualitative accounts of "how things work." Finally, information about program outcomes can also be quantitative in nature (for example, data on how many clients leave TANF for employment and whether family incomes increase after leaving TANF) or qualitative (for example, case studies of how working families' social lives, attitudes and beliefs, or civic engagement have changed since leaving welfare for work).

PRINTED MATERIAL

Often the first and easiest information to collect for an implementation study is contained in existing documents. These sources are particularly useful when researching the origins and development of a program design, or when describing the program model, how the program is supposed to operate, and the program's overall goals and performance measures. Depending on where and how the program was developed, useful summaries of program rationale, resource requirements, and goals may be found in legislative documents and agency budget documents.

In addition to documenting a program's development, design, and goals, printed material is also a useful source of detailed information about a how a program is supposed to operate. Common sources of this information are worker manuals and client instructional material, including texts and learning aids used in various services and activities. Also important are program forms and client notices, as well as administrative letters to program management and staff.

Prepared statistical reports, including background data on state and local demographic and socioeconomic conditions and trends, as well as routine and ad hoc program statistical reports, represent another important type of printed material. Reports that summarize chart trends in client characteristics, activities, and outcomes are particularly useful.

Documents that may be needed for an implementation study include the following:

- Program development and planning documents, such as minutes of planning meetings, memoranda related to program development from various departments or other agencies or interest groups, and draft versions of program design;

- Legislation related to program design, goals, benchmarks, operations, and funding;
- Agency budget submissions;
- Program manuals and guidebooks, including program policies, rules, and forms;
- Public information and education materials, including notices and brochures as well as instructional materials associated with key activities (such as client assessments, orientations, job clubs, and services such as child care, career counseling, and job matching);
- Background statistical data, including local and regional economic and demographic conditions and trends;
- Administrative and statistical program reports summarizing program activities, clients' status, progress to date and progress against established benchmarks; and
- Public information materials and relevant newspaper articles.

Some typical sources for the documentary material listed above may include the following:

- Specific agency divisions, such as those dealing with policies and procedures, or agency budget offices;
- Legislative libraries and information offices;
- Agency research and statistics offices;
- Local newspaper archives; and
- Background statistical material from other agencies, such as the state employment security division.

In the past, much of the material listed above was only available as hard copy. Today, many federal, state, and local agencies are increasingly making these materials available online on agency web sites accessible to the public. The Internet is often a good place to begin a document search for material relevant to an implementation study.

ADMINISTRATIVE DATA

Administrative data are normally collected and maintained as part of ongoing program and agency operations. Administrative data are particularly valuable sources of information about client characteristics related to eligibility and grant levels, participation patterns, benefit histories, service use, and other program experiences. Moreover, within the limits imposed by available automated data, administrative data allow researchers to focus on individual clients, families, specific groups of clients, or the caseload as a whole.

Administrative systems used for welfare reform programs include both hard-copy and automated data. Hard-copy administrative data may include, for example, client applications and other printed forms, as well as case narratives and records of client activities, benchmarks, and program outcomes (such as reasons for program exits).[1] Because hard-copy data tend to include more information than is entered into automated systems, hard-copy data are often useful sources of information about the details of administrative processes and individual client and family situations and program experiences. Moreover, the many forms, program letters, and case narratives often included in client files offer the potential to reconstruct a "program history" for an individual client or family.[2] Finally, because some data entered on the automated files may get erased or overwritten over time, the hard-copy files have the potential to allow a more complete historical reconstruction of a family's situation at program entry and their complete program experience. Because locating, organizing, and abstracting hard-copy files can be labor intensive, however, they are rarely used in sample sizes large enough to make statistical generalizations about a program's participants. More often, hard-copy files are used to support intensive case studies of individual clients or families, or of small groups of clients and families.

In contrast to hard-copy files, the data found in automated administrative systems are relatively inexpensive to organize and manipulate in developing descriptive statistics about a program's caseload. They differ from hard-copy data files in at least two important ways. First, unlike hard-copy files, which ideally contain some record of any program events that produced a piece of paper, the data normally found online in automated administrative systems represent a snapshot, or cross section, of current program status. This is due in large part to the fact that these systems were primarily designed to assist eligibility workers in program administration rather than for program research or evaluation. The data found in welfare administrative systems are thus usually those associated with program eligibility and grant level (for example, family size and total income), those associated with behavioral requirements (for example, the ages of children in the household, which may affect the obligation of adult case members to work or prepare for work), and those indicating recent program benefit transactions. Because most states archive some part of the administrative record each month, however, automated administrative data may be used either to characterize the caseload at a point in time or to create a historical, or longitudinal, record of changes over time.[3]

A second difference between hard copy and automated administrative files is that the automated files usually include summary data. For example, while an eligibility form may include detailed information on all sources of family income and work-related expenses, the automated data may only include the results of the calculations needed to determine eligibility and calculate grant levels.

The fact that automated systems primarily support program administration also affects the reliability and usefulness of some system data. Data directly tied to some aspect of program eligibility, status (such as "exempt" or "nonexempt" work registrant, for example), or grant level, are usually more reliable than data either tangentially related or unrelated to program status. The automated data on family income, household composition, and disability status, for example, are usually more complete and reliable than automated data on education or work history, or the precise reasons for program exits. Eligibility workers with large caseloads often cannot or do not take the time to gather these other data or to treat them with the same care afforded eligibility- and benefit-related family information.

For implementation research on welfare reform programs, the most commonly mined automated administrative system is the one used for the TANF program, usually the best source for summary information on program participation data, benefits, and client family characteristics and eligibility factors. The TANF administrative system often also includes information about participation in the Food Stamp program and at least information about eligibility for Medicaid, if not more detailed information on Medicaid utilization. Most state welfare departments produce monthly statistical summaries of selected information from their administrative systems, such as the number of families entering and leaving the TANF roles, the number of TANF families with earned income, and average TANF grants.

Although the automated administrative systems offer a more efficient source of data on large numbers of clients than do hard-copy files, manipulating the automated data can command relatively large resources. This is again due in part to the fact that the systems are primarily designed to aid in the administration of individual clients and individual cases and not for research. Because of the potentially large expense in collecting, reorganizing, and analyzing the automated data, implementation studies should consider carefully whether or not the statistical information required for a specific research question or goal can be provided by regular monthly statistical reports normally produced by the TANF agency.

Another limitation of administrative data is that they track clients only while clients are actively on the rolls. Other large-scale administrative systems are often used in implementation research both to collect nonprogram data about clients and data about clients during periods when their cases are inactive.[4] For example, the Child Support Enforcement program administrative system (often separate from, but linked to, the system used for TANF) includes information about the legal status of children with absent parents and the support income contributed by absent parents, whether or not children or parents are receiving financial assistance. The state's child welfare system also includes information about children that have had contact with child protective services. The administrative system containing state quarterly employment and wage data (which tracks most employment, regardless of TANF program status), is a valuable independent source of information about reported earnings during, before, or after spells on the TANF program.[5]

To summarize, administrative data used in implementation research may include the following:

- Hard-copy case files, including client forms and notices; detailed accounts of client background and circumstances; and program experiences and outcomes. Because collecting information from case files is labor intensive, these data are most useful to create individual family histories or profiles, rather than to develop statistical information for large groups of clients.
- Automated computer files, including data on client history and characteristics related to eligibility and grant levels, program benefits, current program status, and behavioral requirements. These data are most convenient for developing summary statistical profiles of large groups of clients both at a point in time and over time, rather than for collecting comprehensive program histories of individual clients or families.

Some common sources of administrative data associated with participants in welfare programs include the following:

- TANF program hard-copy files; employment and training service provider hard-copy files;
- TANF program automated administrative systems (usually also include information about Food Stamp and Medicaid programs);
- Quarterly wage-reporting system (established for administration of the Unemployment Insurance program);
- Administrative systems for the Child Support Enforcement program;
- Administrative systems for the Workforce Investment Act (WIA) program.

INDIVIDUAL AND GROUP OPEN-ENDED ORAL ACCOUNTS, DESCRIPTIONS, OPINIONS, AND RECOMMENDATIONS

An important staple of implementation research are first-hand accounts of what is happening in a program by people directly involved in program design, management, or operations, including clients and their families. Because such accounts are usually developed during conversations with researchers, and not by short answer questionnaires, they are often referred to as "open ended." Gathering such information from limited numbers of key informants is usually inexpensive and quick, and is probably the most widely used data collection strategy in implementation research. Individual and group accounts of program experiences can have multiple purposes in the context of implementation research. For example, the most direct and probably most common use of first-hand accounts is to develop initial models of how things actually work in the program. With this goal in mind, key informants, usually program management and staff, are generally asked to describe what they do and how they do it. When the questions are restricted to informants' direct program responsibilities and experiences, responses may be accepted at face value.

A second purpose of first-hand accounts is to collect opinions of those involved in the program about how well things are working, why things are working as they are, and how to improve program operations and results. In this respect, key informants are used as first-level program evaluators. For example, caseworkers' opinions about how useful a new eligibility form is for program administration might be considered more valid than their opinions about the effectiveness of job clubs provided by other agencies. Similarly, clients' opinions about how useful a particular service has been in helping them gain employment are probably more valid indications of the true value of the service than the opinions of the staff directing the club. Note, however, that even when the evaluative judgments of key informants are restricted to areas of expertise or first-hand experience, they are individual and subjective. Nevertheless, the opinions of those most affected by program design and operations are valuable indices of program satisfaction and thus important signs of program success.

A third important purpose of individual and group accounts within the context of implementation research is to gain some insight into the prevailing institutional culture of the program and the attitudes of program stakeholders toward the program, its goals, and its services. In this application, the subjects being interviewed are more the objects of inquiry than primary sources of information about the program. In this mode, implementation research can take on the flavor of ethnography, in which the program is understood within the context of the social life of its actors. This aspect of implementation research can be an indispensable tool for interpreting program experiences and understanding program effectiveness and outcomes.

Data from individual and group oral accounts may include the following examples:

- First-hand accounts of how things work in the program and other relevant descriptive information;
- Key informants' judgments about how well the program is designed or operating and recommendations for change; and
- Information about key informants' beliefs, motivations, and behaviors that help flesh out the social and psychological context in which the program operates.

Some typical key informants for implementation studies of welfare reform programs include the following:

- Program applicants, clients, and former clients;
- State- and local-level TANF program management and staff; other relevant agency management and staff;
- Service provider management and staff; and
- Representatives of public interest and advocacy groups.

OBSERVATIONS OF PROGRAM ACTIVITIES AND SERVICES

Although much information may be available from the accounts of those involved in program activities, implementation researchers often need to observe program processes and activities in order to gain some first-hand knowledge of the program and to put oral accounts in perspective. Depending on the number of observations and the manner in which program events are sampled, it is potentially possible to develop statistically meaningful measures, or ratings, of those events. In most implementation research, however, observations are used to develop more impressionistic, qualitative information to supplement the first-hand oral accounts from program actors.

Some common program events or activities often observed in implementation studies of welfare reform programs include the following:

- Initial eligibility and redetermination interviews;
- Individual and group program orientations;
- Employability assessments and service referrals;
- Education and employment services, such as job-finding classes, job-club meetings and activities, and vocational training classes; and
- Job counseling and job referral meetings.

DATA FROM SURVEYS AND PROGRAM QUESTIONNAIRES

Sometimes implementation studies require systematic and consistent data from large numbers of informants that are not included in administrative systems. For example, studies concerned with developing statistical generalizations about in-program and post-program client characteristics, experiences, and outcomes require comparable information from sufficiently large samples of individuals. Open-ended interviews may neither be feasible for the sample sizes needed, nor easily coded or appropriate for statistical analysis. Survey questionnaires are a convenient way to ask the same questions in the same way to multiple informants; precoded and short-answer questionnaires are more easily handled in statistical analysis. Moreover, post-program data about one-time clients are limited through nonwelfare administrative systems.[6] Some survey data are required if a study is to learn about a wide range of outcomes for ex-clients.

Implementation studies may also require information about program management and staff, such as their knowledge of program policies and services, or their understanding and internalization of program philosophy and culture. This information is simply not available through administrative systems or other secondary sources. To some degree, implementation research can collect fleshed out, if anecdotal, information about these areas through the open-ended interviews described above. But if researchers wish to characterize the knowledge and opinions of a large group of individuals, the most efficient method is to use some form of standardized survey. The same rationale holds for studies that need to gauge public opinion and acceptance of welfare reform policies and goals.

Survey information may include, for example,

- Client background information;
- Client program participation patterns and use of services;
- Client knowledge and opinions of program polices, activities, and services;
- Client outcomes;
- Staff knowledge and opinions of program policies, activities, services, and goals; and
- General public knowledge and opinion of program policies, goals, and results.

Data Collection Strategies: General Considerations

The variety of specific questions that implementation research addresses requires several types of data and multiple data collection and organization strategies. However, not every implementation study needs to use every strategy. For example, the goals of a specific study may be limited and may lead to a narrow set of questions requiring only some types of data. Moreover, the same research question may be addressed by one or more types of data, depending on the requirements of the program design, its administration, and management decisions. Although data sources and collection strategies may differ from study to study, implementation research strives to maximize data accuracy, representativeness, and comparability.

DATA ACCURACY

The usefulness of an implementation study for program design and management is in large part based on the accuracy of its findings. If the researchers fail to "get it right," program managers and policymakers may make decisions based on incorrect information; legislators, interest groups, and the public may base opinions about program performance on faulty findings. A major part of "getting it right" is basing program descriptions and analyses on reliable data.

Data collected for implementation research may be inaccurate and unreliable for several reasons. Sometimes, the data are simply wrong. For example, the data about client characteristics contained in administrative systems may be inaccurate due to carelessness by intake workers or data entry clerks or because of wrong information provided by program applicants and clients. Summary statistical reports may be based on poor information or may be the result of poor or faulty statistical methods. An informant's account of some process or activity may be incomplete, or may be based on mistaken ideas about what workers generally do or about what the most up-to-date policies and procedures are. Sometimes the information collected may be biased or colored by the informant's subjective opinions, prejudices, or self-interest. For example, a manager's response to questions about what is working well and what is not may be swayed by fears of exposing some weaknesses in local office administration that may be attributed to poor management. Similarly, a client's response to certain survey questions may be influenced by notions of what the "right" answer should be (as opposed to the honest or accurate answer) or by some interest in withholding information.

Maximizing data accuracy is a key aspect of implementation research design. There are several strategies researchers may employ. For example, when multiple sources of information exist about purely factual information, such as the size of a particular family's TANF grant or an individual's earnings, the best strategy is to rely on the primary source of data as much as possible. The most accurate source of information on TANF grants is likely the administrative record, which is directly linked to the check or bank account deposit provided to the client. Similarly, the quarterly wage system is usually considered to be a more accurate source of information about earnings than client surveys, since employers report earnings directly to the quarterly wage system.[7]

Another general rule for data on simple facts for which there is one correct answer is to rely on only one source.[8] If the study cannot use the primary source for some reason, the next best source should be used. But it is a mistake to think that you can "home in" on the right answer to a purely factual question by getting many different answers from many different sources. As a colleague of mine likes to say, "a man with two watches doesn't know what time it is."

Questions for which there is only one correct answer should not be confused with questions for which multiple correct answers may exist. Questions with multiple correct answers often come into play in implementation studies that describe "how things work" simply because things may work differently in different times, in different places, and when done by different individuals. An example of such a question is "How does the TANF eligibility process work?" (as opposed to "How is the TANF eligibility process supposed to work?"). The answer to the question may be different for different workers, supervisory units, and local offices.

The usual way to increase data reliability in these instances is to ask multiple respondents the same question. This approach is particularly useful when collecting information about program processes and events. For example, a common strategy in collecting descriptive data about how the TANF eligibility process works is to ask a number of different informants (for example, several intake workers and several supervisors) about the process. When sorting through the multiple responses, researchers tend to trust the more consistent responses across informants and mistrust divergent responses. The idea is not necessarily to generate an "average" description from informants' accounts, but to generate a consistent description and to be able to recognize accounts that differ from the consistent description. The goal is to describe how things *usually* work and any important variations.

Another way to improve the reliability of data collected from open-ended interviews or surveys is to refine the way in which the question is asked or the issue is discussed. In open-ended interviews, for example, any ambiguous or inconsistent answers should be clarified through probes and follow-up questions. This strategy should at least ensure that the informant's responses are clear and consistent. Similarly, surveys should be designed to minimize confusion about the intent of the question. Although good survey design may not necessarily increase the probability that respondents will be truthful, it should reduce the number of answers that are ambiguous or incorrect because of respondent confusion or misunderstanding (see the discussion below on designing surveys).

REPRESENTATIVENESS OF THE DATA

Another important goal of data collection is to achieve representativeness, or "external validity." This is the issue of how typical the data collected are of conditions elsewhere and at other times. Are program operations in a particular local office or group of offices typical of how things are done elsewhere? Are the employment outcomes for TANF clients in June and July representative of outcomes over the entire year? Just as findings about program design and operations should be based on accurate data, they should also be based on representative data.

The usual way that researchers try to ensure a given level of representativeness is to apply the principles of sampling statistics when choosing how many and which "units" (such as TANF clients, eligibility workers, or local offices, for example) should be used as data sources. A major goal of the sampling strategy is to attain an acceptable "confidence level" that the data collected from the sample will be representative of the group as a whole. Although there are many factors to consider, in general the larger the sampled group (assuming the sampling is random), the more representative the findings and the more confident policymakers and program operators can be in using the findings to make decisions.

Implementation studies that are purely exploratory—for example, that are aimed at uncovering the variety of situations, problems, or solutions surrounding the introduction of new programs, policies, or services— usually do not have to worry about representativeness of findings. Their goal is simply to discover "what's going on out there." It is only when those studies try to characterize and assess the overall implementation and performance of the new program that the issue of representativeness arises.

Data Comparability

An issue related to data validity is data comparability. The same data items should be consistent and comparable across different researchers and different data sources. There are reasons, however, why this may not always be the case. For example, individuals responding to open-ended questions or survey items may understand or interpret those questions in different ways. Moreover, different researchers may conduct open-ended interviews differently and may understand and record responses differently. When data are not comparable and consistent, answers that appear to be the same may mean something different; conversely, data items that appear to be different may actually be similar. Serious inconsistencies in data collection can lead to faulty conclusions.

A number of general strategies for maximizing data comparability are available. One is to develop instruments that are sufficiently detailed and clear to minimize misunderstanding or ambiguity. This is particularly important when designing telephone or in-person survey questionnaires, as interviewers usually simply ask the questions as scripted and do not customize lengthy explanations for each respondent. Open-ended interview protocols may include standard clarifying prompts or explanations for the interviewer for particularly complex topics or complicated questions. A second rule is to use the same data collection strategy for the same data. For example, if a study relies on the quarterly wage reporting system to measure TANF family earnings, it should not use data on earnings from client surveys or other sources.[9] Another important tool for maintaining data comparability across researchers or data collectors is thorough and consistent training, including the use of manuals that have question-by-question explanations and rationales. The comparability of data from open-ended interviews or focus groups can sometimes also be improved after data collection in discussions among the field researchers (see chapter 3).

The Cost of Data Collection

Like most research, implementation research must consider tradeoffs given the time and resources allowed for the study. Because implementation research potentially requires a great variety and amount of data, and because the research results may be expected to provide guidance for policymakers and program operators within short time frames, researchers must often make compromises on the amount, quality, and type of data collected. Some data collection strategies may be rejected in favor of less optimal methods simply because of the expense and time involved in pursuing the best strategies.

One important tradeoff in data collection is between the "depth" and the sample size of the data. "Depth," in this context, means the level of detail in qualitative data or the number of variables included in quantitative data. Sample size is the number of units (such as the number of clients, eligibility workers, or local TANF offices) included in the data collection effort. Within a fixed budget and schedule for the research, increases in depth typically imply decreases in sample size, and vice versa.

A study exploring the lives of TANF clients and ex-clients in detail, and seeking to understand what lies "beyond the numbers," may choose a data collection strategy that includes repeated, intensive open-ended interviews with those individuals and their families. This in-depth approach limits the number of individuals and families that may be studied, however. On the other hand, an implementation study that seeks a generalized description of how clients fare after leaving TANF would require greater breadth in the number of individuals covered by the data, but researchers would not normally expect to learn as much about each individual or family in the study sample as in the in-depth study. Table 2.1 shows how the tradeoffs between depth and sample size are implied by four alternative sources of data about TANF clients: standard statistical reports, administrative systems, surveys, and in-depth open-ended interviews.

How do researchers make decisions about a study's data needs and about the inevitable tradeoffs in selecting data collection methods? Perhaps the most important guide is the underlying purpose of the study. For example, implementation studies that are exploratory in nature tend to require more depth to reduce the chances of missing something important in the data collection effort. On the other hand, studies primarily measuring the degree to which the program is operating and performing as planned (for example, "How well is the program being implemented across the state and where are the problems or exemplary program sites?") probably require larger sample sizes and may need to compromise on depth by measuring a limited number of summary variables across a relatively large number of clients, workers, and/or local offices. Once a decision is made about the basic nature of the study—exploratory or definitive—specific data needs follow from the study's research questions.[10]

Conducting Interviews and Observations on Site

The data that may be required for an implementation study are varied and call for a range of collection strategies. Some data may be collected electronically, by mail, or telephone. Other data collection efforts—such as in-depth open-ended interviews, focus groups, and observations, for example—require an in-person approach. Most thorough implementation studies require researchers to spend some amount of time "in the field," or at the location where the program is administered, where services are delivered, or where clients work and live. This section summarizes how to organize fieldwork and how to collect data in the field.[11]

Table 2.1. *Tradeoffs between Depth and Breadth in Data Sources and Collection*

Less expensive per unit— Less depth			More expensive per unit— More depth
Standard statistical reports include data on limited number of variables based on administrative data averaged across relatively large groups; characterize individuals and families during spells on TANF.	*Administrative systems* include data on limited number of variables but more than statistical reports; include comparable microdata for each individual and family; characterize individuals and families during spells on TANF.	*Surveys* include data on variables needed specifically for research study; include comparable microdata for each individual and family surveyed; characterize individuals and families during times on and off TANF.	*In-depth open-ended interviews* include data on variables needed specifically for research study; interviews allow for probes and discussions tailored to each individual or family's unique situation; characterize individuals and families during times on and off TANF.
Larger sample size			*Smaller sample size*
Standard statistical reports include summary data based on entire state TANF caseload (usually also available at county or local administrative district level); series of reports (usually monthly) allow for convenient view of trends over relatively long time periods.	*Administrative systems* include microdata on currently and recently active TANF caseload; online automated data limited in historical scope.	*Surveys* include microdata on representative sample of defined group.	*In-depth open-ended interviews* include in-depth data on limited group of families; sample may or may not include special types of individuals or families, but is rarely large enough to be considered representative of some larger group.

Planning On-Site Interviews and Observations

Before organizing the on-site data collection effort of an implementation study, researchers must make a number of decisions, including the following examples.

Which respondents to interview and which activities to observe. Depending on the general and specific research goals generated by an implementation study, what type of individuals should be interviewed or organized into focus groups, and which activities, events, or services should be observed? For a comprehensive implementation study that seeks to understand the design, development, introduction, ongoing administration, and results of a new program or service, the list can be large. For example, targeted respondents could include the following: state-level TANF agency management and staff; management and staff of related state social service and employment agencies; state legislators and staff; representatives of the state executive branch; local TANF agency management and staff; management and staff of related local social service agencies; representatives of service providers; representatives of local employers or business groups; representatives of statewide and local public interest and advocacy groups; and TANF clients and ex-clients and their families.

Activities or services observed could include, for example, intake interviews, redetermination interviews, employment program orientations and assessments, job clubs and other job-finding group and individual activities or services, skills training classes, program exit interviews, and time-limit or sanction appeals sessions.

For studies that are more focused on specific issues, the target respondents should be those with first-hand experience of the issue. For example, an investigation of how the TANF application process works would normally gather information from applicants, clerks, and eligibility workers and supervisors. Similarly, information about how employability assessments are conducted should be obtained from TANF clients and the case managers or employment specialists that normally conduct the assessments.

How many and which "units" to interview or observe. Parallel to the issue of which type of individual or event to interview and observe is the issue of how many of those "units of analysis" to choose and how to choose among all potential units. This is the problem of sampling strategy, and it is guided in part by the overall purpose of the study. For example, for a purely exploratory study that seeks to learn "what sorts of things are happening" in the implementation of a new program, one strategy might be to interview or observe a small number of units, but to choose units that are likely to represent some variation, such as local offices in different regions of the state, or TANF families with different demographic characteristics. This approach helps increase the chance of observing different implementation experiences and can then inform a more systematic study.

A study that seeks to characterize the average features or outcomes of a program, or to assess the prevalence of some pattern across many workers or local offices, faces the issue of selecting a representative sample of the units to be characterized or assessed. For a given level of precision, sampling statistics may be used to estimate how many of the analysis units should be contacted. In general, a larger sample with less variation among the units will yield more precise and more representative estimates. The research profession has traditional standards of precision that are high and often require large samples. However, useful information to support design or management decisions can certainly be based on smaller samples, with the caveat that the smaller the sample, the higher the risk that the derived estimates will deviate from the truth. There is no sharp distinction between a collection of anecdotes and an estimate based on a scientific sample, but only gradations of statistical precision. These considerations about smaller samples often come into play with fieldwork because it can be very expensive and impractical to conduct long interviews with many respondents.

The decision of which units should be sampled is usually made separately and before the decision about how many units to sample. The answer to the former question is not always straightforward, but depends in part on guesses about where the most variation occurs. For example, if a study wants to assess the degree to which workers and applicants discuss relevant employment services during the eligibility interview, the sampling strategy should be guided by whether the bigger differences in practice are among individual workers, individual supervisory units, or individual offices. The most effective strategy would be to sample at the level of the unit with the largest amount of variation.

Designing interviews for the field. Decisions about the type of information needed affect how interviews should be conducted in the field. For example, if researchers have few preconceived ideas about how a new program or service has been implemented, the instruments used to guide interviews and observations are likely to be less structured and more open-ended, focusing on general topics. On the other hand, if researchers have a detailed model of the program as a reference, the interviews and observations can be guided by more structured instruments that make reference to specific procedures and policies and that include prompts based on known details. Finally, the most structured interviews provide for short-answer or precoded responses that are most easily quantified.

Another important decision that affects the design and conduct of the interviews is whether to treat respondents primarily as informants for descriptions of program features and activities or to treat respondents themselves as objects of inquiry. In the former instance, interviews are more likely to proceed like conversations, as the interviewer introduces general topics and probes for more details and clarifications. When the object of the interview is to collect information about the respondent's experiences, assessments, or recommendations, however, it is important that the interviewer refrain from leading the respondent with suggestive probes or reactions to the responses. Also, there are likely to be more structured questions and close-ended responses. Because many interviews conducted in the field have two goals—to gather descriptive information about the program and to describe and assess the respondents themselves—it is often useful to design interview guides that distinguish between the two approaches according to the purpose of each question. One way to keep the two styles separate is to begin with purely fact-finding questions and close the interview with questions about the respondents and their opinions.

Preparing for field visits. Because fieldwork is costly and, depending on the range of activities on site, may draw on the time and resources of program management and staff, as well as on the time of TANF applicants, clients, or ex-clients, careful and thorough preparation is important. The following is a list of activities that should be carried out prior to fieldwork:

- *Gaining clearance and informing sites.* Even if no formal interviews are conducted, most visits to state or local TANF agencies or service-provider sites require advance notice and clearance. Usually, clearance begins at the highest level of the agency under study. If the client is the TANF agency itself, of course, clearance may not be a problem when visiting local TANF offices. However, upper-level permission may be required if other agencies or service providers will be visited for the study. Also, even if clearance may not be needed for visits to the TANF agency, directors of local TANF offices to be visited should be notified well before the site visit. A common approach is to send letters signed by the client agency's director (e.g., the commissioner of the TANF agency), informing other agencies and local TANF offices about the study and that someone from the study will be contacting them about arranging for a visit.

- *Establishing an on-site contact person.* One effective strategy for fieldwork is to request that each site (each local agency office, service provider agency, or training site, for example) designate a staff member to act as a contact for the study. The contact would be a liaison between the site and the study and would be the normal communication link between the two. The site contact can help identify specific respondents, locate needed documents, help arrange and schedule interviews and observations, and distribute any study materials to on-site respondents. Depending on the level of effort required, the site contact may also be asked to help recruit staff or clients for focus groups.

- *Arranging for and scheduling interviews and observations on-site.* On-site interviews and observations should be scheduled several weeks in advance of the visit. One effective approach is to draw up a tentative schedule, indicating the individual or type of respondent and the approximate length of time for the interview. The tentative schedule should be sent to the site contact who then attempts to fill interview slots with the appropriate individuals. The schedule should be flexible, so that the site contact can fit the needs of the study with respondents' schedules and work demands.

- *Sending materials in advance of the site visit.* Depending upon the specific purpose of the interview (or set of questions), it is often a good idea to send the interview or topic guides in advance of the site visit. In particular, for example, when the major purpose of the interview is descriptive, having the interview or topic guide beforehand can help prepare respondents for the interview. Often, informants will jot down notes and collect useful information relating to topics to be covered in the interview. Sending materials prior to field visits is also helpful for the parts of the interview dealing with informants' opinions and recommendations. Particularly in instances when the study is more interested in considered and supported opinions and assessments, rather than in "snap judgments," it is helpful to allow time for informants to reflect before the interview.

In two situations, at least, it is probably not a good idea to send interview guides or questionnaires to informants before conducting the interview. For example, when part of the purpose of the interview is to assess management or staff knowledge of new policies or services, tipping them off to the questions in advance will clearly undermine that goal. A more subtle case in which the interview or topic guide should not be sent in advance is when informants may be tempted to discuss their answers in advance and influence each other or develop a "company line" response to particular questions. For questions eliciting opinions and recommendations, this risk should be weighed against the benefits of more thoroughly prepared responses.

Whether or not a study team decides to send complete or partial interview or observation instruments in advance, at a minimum an information sheet explaining the study, the purpose of the visit, the conduct of the interview, and an example of some of the topics to be covered should be made available to all prospective informants before the site visit.

- *Staff training and preparation.* A final and critical activity for larger studies that involve multiple researchers visiting multiple sites is staff training and preparation. Although any implementation study should be staffed by experienced and knowledgeable researchers, thorough training in the overall purpose and approach of the study, as well as in the specific purpose and range of expected responses to each question or data need, is indispensable. First, thorough training fills in any gaps in relevant program or policy knowledge needed to conduct the interviews, understand responses, and grasp when to probe for clarification or additional information. Second, the training also maximizes the comparability of collected data by communicating a consistent message concerning the meaning of each question to all researchers.

  Staff training, site visit preparation, and post-visit activities are often organized by a study manual. The manual and the training usually cover the following topics:
  - Overview of the design and administration of program or policies studied, including a glossary of terms likely to be encountered on site;
  - Overview of the study design and goals, and how site visits relate to the study;

○ Overview of data collection activities on site, including hard-copy material to be collected, activities to be observed, individuals and groups to be interviewed, and overall data collection responsibilities;

○ Pre-visit preparation and site communications;

○ Behavior and etiquette on site;

○ Conducting the interviews, including a detailed discussion of the intention, goals, and expected range of responses on a question-by-question ("Q by Q") basis;

○ Taking notes and keeping a record of the interviews; and,

○ Post-visit activities, including organizing and reporting responses and other data, and circumstances governing post-visit contact with informants.

Figure 2.1 presents the contents of a training manual for the fieldwork in a multistate implementation study of the Low-Income Child Care program.

- *Post-visit activities.* Site visitors usually have several activities to complete once the field visit is over. For example, interview notes have to be organized and put into a form that is accessible to other study staff. Each question or topic in the interview or observation guides must be addressed; if there is no answer to the question or item, the researcher should explain why. Further, after thorough review of interview notes, site visitors should expect to conduct follow-up telephone calls to informants for clarification or missing details. Finally, as described in greater detail below, site visitors should meet to compare their findings and experiences and to begin the process of analyzing data.

Collecting Data On Site

Major in-person, on-site data collection activities include open-ended interviews and observations. Although other forms of data collection may take place on site—such as focus groups, ethnographic studies, survey questionnaires, and case record abstractions—those activities are usually conducted by specialists, rather than by typical implementation study field workers. This section discusses how to go about designing and conducting open-ended interviews and structured observations.

Figure 2.1. *Fieldwork Training Manual Contents*

**Outline of Training Manual for the National Study of
Child Care for Low-Income Families:
State and Community Study**

**Chapter 1: Introduction to the National Study of Child Care for
Low-Income Families**
A. Purpose and organization of the training manual
B. Overview of the study
C. Objectives and design of the state and community study;
    relationship to overall research objectives
D. Project schedule and deliverables

**Chapter 2: Overview of Data Collection Requirements for the State
and Community Study**
A. Summary of required data and collection strategies (matrix)
B. Pre–field visit data collection
C. Informant interviews and other field activities
D. Post-visit follow-up data collection and clarification

Chapter 3: Pre–Field Visit Preparations and Data Collection
A. Studying abstracted information and state and community profiles
B. Arranging appointments and sending site profiles to informants

**Chapter 4: Conducting the Interviews: Question-by-Question
Discussion**
A. Introduction: techniques for conducting open-ended interviews
B. Conducting the interview of state child care subsidy agency
    informants
C. Conducting the interview of state informants for child care quality
    improvements
D. Conducting the interview of state TANF agency informants
E. Conducting the interview of county child care subsidy agency

Source: Extract from unpublished fieldwork training manual, Abt Associates' study of the Low-Income Child Care Program.

Developing instruments for open-ended interviews. The usual instrument for conducting open-ended interviews in the field is an interview guide. Interview guides can range in length and complexity from a simple one-page list of discussion topics for each interview to a multipage compendium of scripted questions with prompts and probes specifically tailored to a type of informant (such as a TANF eligibility worker). While a simple topic list may be a quick and convenient way to get into the field, it has some important drawbacks for a systematic study. First, the interviewer may forget or pass over some potentially important details within a given topic. Second, the treatment of each topic will likely differ across researchers and perhaps across respondents, possibly resulting in a loss of data comparability. Using a structured interview guide can help increase the comprehensiveness, completeness, and comparability of data.

Two primary and related design issues for interview instruments are which topics to include and how to customize the topic areas and their treatment for different types of respondents. For example, it is not likely that questions about program design will be included in an interview guide for an eligibility worker. Moreover, although both an eligibility worker and a state TANF agency director may be asked questions about client responses to a new program or policy, the specific follow-up questions and probes will likely be different for the two respondents. For illustrative purposes, we use the example of an eligibility worker for a TANF program with a "Work First" design that stresses a rapid move into a job over longer-term training and work preparation.

A convenient place to start constructing the interview is to make a list of the topics you want to cover. Two important criteria for the topic list include: (1) are the topics directly related to the informant's likely scope of knowledge, and (2) are the topics related to the study's research questions? An interview with a TANF eligibility worker in the context of a comprehensive implementation study of a state's TANF program might include the following topic areas: worker background and experience; worker training for the new program or policy; program startup; TANF application process; applicant and client behavioral requirements; applicant and client education, training, and work-related services; applicant and client supportive services; managing and monitoring cases; time limits and transitional procedures and services; and overall program assessment and recommendations.

A convenient next step in developing interview guides is to list the issues to be covered under each topic heading. For example, for the topic area "applicant and client education, training, and work-related ser-vices," issues to be covered may include the following: range of services available; access to services; content, intensity, and duration of services; adequacy and quality of services; service providers; and communication with service providers.

The list of more detailed issues then becomes the basis for developing specific questions, prompts, and probes. For example, a group of open-ended questions focused on the issues of "content, intensity, and dura-tion of services" and "adequacy and quality of services" might look like the sequence in figure 2.2 (note that instructions to the interviewer are in parentheses).

Although in developing a full set of interview guides (or topic lists), researchers may want to create a guide for each type of respondent, some topics and some specific questions may be the same across respondents. Where appropriate, the use of the same topics or questions for a variety of informants allows for some analysis of differences in responses by staff or management function.

Conducting the interviews. Researchers using open-ended interview guides should expect to encounter a wide range of personalities and speaking styles among their informants. As the goal of any interview is to elicit answers to the questions and to collect as much relevant informa-tion as possible from each informant, field researchers must learn to adapt to the conversational style of informants. In particular, it is impor-tant to keep the conversation on the topic at hand and to keep the inter-view within the scheduled time slot. Although part of the purpose of an open-ended interview is to allow informants to expand on the issues dis-cussed, as well as for the interviewer to probe for more depth, the inter-viewer should try to remain in control of the interview's pace, length, and subject matter. With some experience, this can be done in a polite and courteous manner.

Although some informants are more naturally forthcoming than others, field researchers should expect respondents to answer the ques-tion that is asked and not necessarily to volunteer any extra information. For this reason, probing questions are very helpful in digging deeper for information that may not appear to be important or relevant to the re-spondent. For example, when asked to explain the behavioral require-ments for TANF applicants and clients, a case manager might neglect to mention all of the situations that may exempt an individual from partici-pation in a work-related activity. The oversight may be due to a memory

Figure 2.2. *Illustrative Questions for Open-Ended Interviews with TANF Case Managers*

Interview Guide for TANF Case Manager

Topic VI: Applicant and client education, training, and work-related services

VI.3: Content, intensity, and duration of services. For each of the education, training, and work-related services available to TANF applicants and clients, please tell me in a few sentences what the service consists of. For example, describe the content of (name each that applies):

> employability assessment
> career exploration
> individual job search and job search assistance
> group job search
> job club
> job referral
> job counseling
> adult basic education
> on-the-job training
> work experience
> vocational education
> workfare
> subsidized employment
> any other relevant service

For each of the services offered, please tell me how long the service typically lasts, as well as the frequency and duration of service sessions.

VI.4: Adequacy and quality of services. For each of the education, training, and work-related services available to TANF applicants and clients, please tell me whether or not the service is adequate, that is, whether or not the service is likely to assist individuals as intended. (Ask about each service listed in VI.3 individually.) How do you know whether or not the service is effective? For example, do you get regular feedback from your clients? Have you observed any of the services for yourself? Do you get feedback from your colleagues and other TANF program staff? If the service is not adequate, why? What would need to be done to improve the service?

For each of the services available, assess the quality of the service. Please tell me if you consider the service to be of high, medium, or low quality. For each assessment, please tell me the grounds for your judgment.

Source: Extract from unpublished interview guide for Abt Associates' evaluation of the To Strengthen Michigan Families Program.

lapse or to a failure to recognize a particular situation as an exemption.[12] To guard against such oversights, the question about exemptions might include lists of common exemptions used elsewhere.

Another useful practice in conducting open-ended interviews is to ask respondents the reasons and/or evidence for their judgmental answers (often, these "challenges" are written in as part of the questions themselves). First, this approach may force informants to think more carefully about their responses and to qualify them in the light of their grounds for holding their opinions. Second, it allows the researcher to weigh the informant's opinion against the strength of the evidence used to support it.

An important issue in conducting on-site interviews concerns how many informants to include in any single interview session. There are some practical tradeoffs in making this decision. Talking to more informants at once can help develop more comprehensive answers, as each informant may fill in gaps in information left by the others. Also, using small group interviews as opposed to individual interviews clearly increases the number of individuals that may be seen during a site visit. On the other hand, however, if there are more than two or three respondents, the researcher can easily lose control of the interview as the interplay among the informants may overpower attempts to focus the conversation on the question at hand. Also, more opinionated informants or informants with stronger personalities may sway the judgments of the others in the group interview.

Confidentiality may be an important issue for open-ended interviews, particularly when informants give their opinions about how well a program or policy is working. For both ethical and legal reasons it is critical to inform respondents about whether and to what degree confidentiality will be protected. Informants' confidence in anonymity (where possible) will also improve the chances for candor in the responses.

Designing and conducting structured observations on site. A clear advantage of fieldwork is the opportunity afforded researchers to observe firsthand critical program events or activities. Just as open-ended interviews require some order to cover required topics and to ensure comparability across interviews and across researchers, so observations benefit from structure. A common tool to use is a list of questions for the observer to answer during or after the activity is observed.

The approach to developing observation guides is similar to the approach for the interview guide. That is, the structured observation guide should be organized around a list of issues related to the content and purpose of the event or activity and should be related to the study's overall goals. The resulting observation guide should be a list of questions that fit one or both of those criteria and that focus and organize the observer's experience in ways useful to the study. Figure 2.3 is an example of an observation guide developed for the evaluation of the To Strengthen Michigan's Families welfare reform demonstration. Observers are expected to answer each question on the guide or explain why the question is not relevant or cannot be answered.

Other Data Collection Activities

On-site open-ended interviews and observations are usually a major part of the data collection effort of an implementation study. As mentioned above, there are many other forms of data and data collection strategies that may be needed to address the varied research requirements of a comprehensive implementation study. Most of the strategies discussed below have been treated extensively in the social science research methods literature (see Charlesworth and Born 2003). This section does not cover them all in depth, but indicates how data collection strategies may be relevant to implementation research and some of the decisions researchers may need to make when adopting the strategies for their projects.

Administrative Data

Administrative data are data normally collected as part of ongoing program administration. Two types are typically available: hard copy and automated.

Collecting hard-copy administrative data. Hard-copy program files may be a source for either quantitative data (such as client characteristics) or discursive data (such as case narratives). The former are usually used by a study to characterize or measure large groups of people, while the latter are most often used in intensive studies of relatively small numbers of individual clients or families. The major challenges to collecting useful and reliable quantitative data from hard-copy files are to locate the necessary forms and other information within each client's files, to select the required data from each paper article, and to record the data in a uniform and well-organized way. Ultimately, these data will likely be entered into a computer for statistical analysis.

Figure 2.3. *Observation Guide*

Observation Guide for Intake and Redetermination Sessions

G1. Time session began: ____:____ AM/PM

G2. Describe the physical setting for the session (e.g., private office, interview space, caseworker's cubicle, etc.).

G3. Has this session been previously scheduled or is the client a "walk-in"?

G4. Describe the client's circumstances. For example, number of children and their ages, employment status, previous receipt of public assistance, etc.

G5. How did the session begin? Did the client appear to be knowledgeable about TANF or TSMF?

G6. How well was the client prepared for the session? Had the client been previously informed about needed information? If so, did the client have all of the necessary information? If not, how did the worker deal with the fact that there was missing information?

G7. How did the session proceed? Was it guided by the application form or did the worker take a different approach?

G8. What information was provided to the client? How detailed were the worker's explanations?

G9. What questions, if any, did the client ask? What was the client's attitude during the session? Did the client appear to understand what the worker said?

G10. Did the client mention being involved in any activities that could be counted towards fulfillment of the Social Contract? If so, what were these activities?

G11. Was the client given any written information during the session? If so, what was the client given? (Researcher: Obtain copies of anything provided to the client.)

G12. What was the result of the session? Was more documentation needed? Could an eligibility determination be made at this point? (If so, was the client eligible/recertified for TANF?)

G13. Time session ended: ____:____ AM/PM

Source: Unpublished observation guide from Abt Associates' evaluation of the To Strengthen Michigan Families Program.

A convenient way to start organizing data collection from hard-copy files is to collect and review standard forms and documents used for program administration. A comparison between the data that are supposed to be collected on the forms and the data that are available on the automated administrative system allows researchers to assess the added value of collecting data from the hard-copy files. The second step in judging the potential usefulness of collecting hard-copy data is to compare the extra information found on the hard-copy data with the data needed to address specific research questions. For example, if an implementation study has as one of its goals an assessment of the match between client education and employment-related needs and recommended program services, the study needs some information about what client information led to the recommended service. While the automated administrative system may indicate the result of the assessment (the recommended service), it is less likely to include the information on which the assessment was based. A thorough evaluation of those decisions would require some details about client characteristics that may be present on the forms used for client assessments.

Once a decision has been made to collect quantifiable data from hard-copy files, the specific data items and source documents need to be identified. Usually, this can be accomplished by reviewing the set of standard forms used in various program activities or events. Because there may be dozens (or over a hundred) forms or information sheets associated with the TANF program, researchers may use worker manuals to target the specific forms that are used to collect the data of interest. Once the program forms have been identified and the specific data items have been chosen, the usual strategy is to design data abstraction forms to record the values for specific data items. An example of a data abstraction form used in a study of the TANF application process is included as figure 2.4.

Collecting data from large numbers of hard-copy files is labor intensive and subject to transcription. Although it is not the most efficient method for collecting statistical data not found on automated systems, it is probably less expensive (though more limited in its scope of data) than client surveys. Another type of information sometimes found in hard-copy files are case narratives.[13] Case narratives are often used in programs or service components with multiple interactions between clients and agency staff, such as child protection cases or intensive skills training programs. The narratives are usually brief descriptions of client activities and progress over time. As such, they can yield valuable data for more intensive

Figure 2.4. *Data Abstraction Form*

Section B: Application Process

B1.   Application date:

___ ___ / ___ ___ / ___ ___
   Month   Day   Year

B2.   Eligibility interview date:

___ ___ / ___ ___ / ___ ___
   Month   Day   Year

Not scheduled..01
Applicant did not attend scheduled interview..02
Information not available.................................98

B3.   Program orientation date:

___ ___ / ___ ___ / ___ ___
   Month   Day   Year

Not applicable..01
Applicant not scheduled for orientation...........02
Applicant scheduled but did not attend...........03
Information not available.................................98

B4.   Was applicant subject to any of the following requirements during the application process?

	Required?			Completed?		
	Yes	*No*	*Info. not available*	*Yes*	*No*	*Info. not available*
a. Job search	1	2	8	1	2	8
b. Job search counseling	1	2	8	1	2	8
c. Employability assessment	1	2	8	1	2	8
d. Sign personal responsibility contract	1	2	8	1	2	8
e. Other (specify:) _____	1	2	8	1	2	8
f. Other (specify:) _____	1	2	8	1	2	8

Source: Extract from unpublished data abstraction form used in Abt Associates' Study of the TANF Application Process.

individual case studies or ethnographic studies of small numbers of clients. Although the case narratives often follow a standardized format, there is much more variation in the quality of these data across caseworkers than for the quantifiable data.

Automated administrative data. Researchers commonly use automated administrative data in implementation studies to measure client characteristics, program benefits and other program events (such as sanctions), program activities and services, and program dynamics (the "flow" of families on and off the TANF rolls). The automated data systems used by TANF programs are large, complex information systems designed primarily for program administration rather than for evaluation research. Nevertheless, the automated administrative data represent the richest, most accessible source of standardized information for all clients during the periods in which they receive TANF benefits. Moreover, because the administrative data are microdata, or related to specific individuals and cases, the data may be manipulated for a variety of statistical analyses.

There are two basic approaches to collecting automated administrative data from state or local TANF agencies. One is to have the TANF agency extract the specific variables for the range of cases needed for the study. This approach avoids some programming labor for the researchers and can yield simplified client records that may be easier to manipulate and analyze. The disadvantage is that the analysis is constrained by the variables chosen beforehand, limiting flexibility. Also, the researchers have less control over the quality of the data extracts, and, if mistakes are made by the TANF agency (and detected), the extracts would have to be provided again. The second, and more usual, approach is to ask the TANF agency to copy the entire administrative system dataset and send the copy to the researchers.[14] This approach allows greater flexibility in choosing appropriate data items for analysis, but usually means more effort in data storage and processing.

For either approach, researchers must take time to learn the structure and content of the administrative system. The system's file layout is a good place to start. This is essentially a roadmap of the data items that the system is designed to record for each individual, case, and household receiving benefits. It is also important to assess beforehand the reliability of the data items that may seem worthwhile to include in the implementation study. Two issues in particular are worth considering.

First, it is important to track any changes in the use of fields on client records. Although states rarely implement an entirely new automated system, they do make frequent changes to their current systems. For example, when a new policy is introduced and requires new data relevant to eligibility status or grant amount, agencies will often "steal" a field in the client record to use to record the new data. Because these changes may not be well documented or because the file layout may not be entirely up to date, it is always a good idea to check any suspect fields with knowledgeable staff.

Second, as discussed above, some automated data not directly associated with eligibility or grant determination data may be missing, incomplete, or inaccurate. Even in systems that have computer "edits" forcing workers to enter some data to change the administrative record, the specific data may be inaccurate. For example, many states require that workers enter a reason for TANF exits before the administrative system will actually close the case and suspend eligibility and benefit payments. In fact, however, workers simply have to enter *some* reason for program exits, even if they do not know the real reason, or if they are in a hurry to finish processing the case change. Studies making extensive use of automated administrative data should probably avoid relying on data that are not used directly for program administration or on data required by computer program edits.

Focus Groups

Focus groups have been used widely in advertising and political consulting for many years, and have more recently made their way into the world of social science research. Focus groups can be very useful in implementation research as *exploratory tools*. The general goal of a focus group is to help uncover and delineate the opinions, concerns, beliefs, and fears of people who share a characteristic or set of characteristics of interest to the research.[15] For example, in an implementation study, the group may be eligibility workers, TANF applicants, or TANF clients who are combining work and welfare. Using a homogenous group of people allows the focus group to outline in depth the ideas and opinions of individuals with a shared set of experiences.

Focus groups are most useful as exploratory strategies because of the largely anecdotal nature of the data they yield. In part, this is because there is no sure way of measuring how representative the discussions are. Even though the group is homogenous across some key characteristics, there is no way of knowing whether the responses of one group of eight or nine individuals would be the same as the responses of other similar groups. Moreover, each focus group may have a unique group dynamic that may shift the discussion in atypical ways, or may be swayed by concerns of that particular day or time. Any one focus group discussion may also be dominated by a few strong personalities that do not accurately represent the group's views.

Uses in implementation research. The focus group's function as an exploratory device yielding largely qualitative, anecdotal information helps define its uses in the context of an implementation study. Usually, focus groups are used to clarify issues prior to other data collection. For example, at the beginning of an implementation study, researchers may use focus groups to gauge the range of reactions from populations affected by the program or policy. Focus groups of eligibility workers or clients subject to the new policies can help researchers decide which questions to ask and what types of responses to expect when planning a more systematic study. Researchers designing a survey of clients who have left the TANF rolls for employment may use focus groups of similar individuals to develop both general topic areas for the survey—such as concerns about child care, transportation, time spent away from home—as well as specific response categories for each issue or question. Similarly, focus groups of workers can help map out the general issues for a worker survey.

Focus groups are also helpful in interpreting information after other data collection has been completed. For example, focus groups are sometimes used to help clarify responses and patterns of responses found in surveys. Particularly in instances in which such responses or patterns are unexpected or counterintuitive, focus groups of survey respondents can be helpful in determining what the responses mean. Another related post–data collection use of focus groups is to "reality-check" narrative descriptions developed from open-ended interviews. This can be particularly valuable when some of the descriptions based on open-ended interviews appear to be eccentric or "outliers." Focus groups of the types of people who were informants for the descriptions may help researchers rule out some accounts as atypical or unusual.

Designing focus groups. Two important design issues for focus groups are what topics to discuss and whom to invite to be in the groups. The choice of topics should always serve the general and specific goals of the study. For example, an implementation study of a Work First program that includes surveys of families who leave TANF for work may organize focus groups of those families to help understand their experiences and the challenges that they face. Similarly, if the Work First program is attempting to change the institutional culture of the TANF office, focus groups of workers might help clarify the range of reactions from workers confronted with a sea change in how "business is done."

The question of whom to invite to focus groups turns on researchers' views of whether there will be important differences in the views, reactions, and beliefs of the various groups affected by the new policy or program. For example, given the importance of child care to TANF clients who must find employment, the study might consider organizing different focus groups for TANF families with preschool children, or for TANF families with no adult available at home to care for children. Similarly, different focus groups of eligibility workers may be organized on the basis of years of service in the TANF agency. The main criterion is whether the specific characteristics of people invited to participate define a group that is likely to have shared opinions and experiences.

A critical tool for conducting a well-organized focus group is the moderator's guide. Depending on the moderator's style and experience, the guide may be as general as a list of topics or as detailed as scripted questions. The important aspect of the guide is to include the range of topics to be discussed. Most guides also include probes to use when the group does not respond to the moderator's questions or topics. An example of part of a focus group moderator's guide for the evaluation of a welfare reform project in Arizona is included as figure 2.5.[16]

Surveys

Surveys are well-established methods of collecting detailed, comparable information from large numbers of individuals. Surveys conducted over the telephone or in person can be relatively expensive and should be used only if needed to address one or more of the research goals. One important criterion for a survey in an implementation study is the need for information that may be generalized over a large group of people. For example, if the study asks what proportion of families leaving the TANF rolls are covered by health insurance, researchers need to ask this question of a sufficiently large sample from that group to be able to make reliable statements about all families leaving TANF.

If researchers need statistical generalizations about groups of individuals or families, a survey may be necessary. That is, if the characteristic or outcome being measured and/or the target group are not included in an available administrative data set, the only way to collect the data is

Figure 2.5. *Focus Group Moderator's Guide*

FOCUS GROUP GUIDE
Group 3: Sanctioned/Benefits Terminated

1. Please think back to the time when you first learned that you might lose your benefits (because you had not complied with the requirements of the JOBS program).

   I'd like each of you, in just a few words, to describe the situation that led to your being sanctioned. I would like to learn how you were notified that you would lose your cash assistance benefits, whether you understood the reason that this was going to happen, and what, if anything, you did right after learning that you would be sanctioned.

   • Did you have a clear understanding of what would happen and why it happened?

   • Did you meet with or try to contact your caseworker to try to resolve the issues that led to your benefits being terminated?

2. Let's take a moment to review. The rules for cash assistance require recipients such as you to cooperate with the JOBS program by taking steps to prepare for work or to find a job. The penalties for not cooperating with the JOBS program involve a gradual reduction of benefits that can lead to a total loss of benefits.

   How many of you feel that this rule is clear? How many of you have been confused at all about this rule? What has been confusing?

   • How much of a factor/reason was your lack of understanding/ confusion about the JOBS requirements in your being sanctioned?

3. Before your benefits were terminated, how concerned were you about the possibility of being sanctioned for not complying with the requirements of the JOBS program?

   If not very concerned: Why weren't you very concerned about being sanctioned?

   ▪ Requirements are easy to meet
   ▪ Little/no verification required
   ▪ Rules aren't strictly enforced
   ▪ Didn't need the benefits that much

Source: Extract from unpublished focus group guide for Abt Associates' evaluation of the Arizona EMPOWER program.

by survey. For example, if the study requires statistical information about the educational level of TANF recipients, it will need to use a survey if the TANF administrative system does not include those data. Similarly, if a study needs statistical information about TANF program leavers, or TANF eligibility workers, it will probably need a survey as comprehensive data about those groups are not likely to be available through administrative data.[17]

Survey content. In part because surveys can be an expensive data collection strategy (particularly if respondent samples are large and include populations that are difficult to locate), and a study often only gets "one shot" at collecting survey data, researchers should take great care in deciding what information the survey should target. As with all data collection, the rationale for any particular question or topic area should come from the research goals and the set of specific research questions for the study. Moreover, it is usually not recommended to rely on surveys for information that may require open-ended answers as opposed to precoded choices. The extra expense associated with post-coding long answers is not likely to be worth the payoff in reliable information.

The most common types of surveys used in implementation studies of welfare reform programs are surveys of clients, applicants, and/or ex-clients; and surveys of welfare program workers and/or management. Surveys of clients, applicants, and/or ex-clients often focus on two general types of data: client characteristics, backgrounds, program experiences, and outcomes; and client opinions, recommendations, and program assessments.

Information about client characteristics, backgrounds, and/or pre-TANF experiences may be needed for an implementation study for a variety of reasons. For example, if the study is interested in focusing on the program and post-program experience of different groups, it may need demographic or socioeconomic data not included in administrative systems. Another related reason to collect these data may be to associate program experiences and outcomes with specific client characteristics in order to refine decisions about policy, resource allocation, and/or program services.

Surveys are sometimes used to gather more information about client program experiences than is included in administrative data. For example, implementation studies measuring the time clients spend attending various services, clients' use of multiple services, or clients' service exit and reentry behaviors may need a survey to supplement or clarify available administrative data. Another type of client behavior sometimes studied in implementation research is "entry" and "exit" decisions, or the reasons clients give when asked about why they applied for welfare and why they decided to leave welfare. Figure 2.6 is an extract from a client survey designed to investigate the decisions and knowledge of clients who were terminated from TANF in Arizona.

Another common use of client surveys is to gather information on customer satisfaction and recommendations for change. This information may indicate whether and to what degree clients feel their needs are being met. It may also help explain clients' in-program behavioral patterns, as well as the relationship between service use and outcomes. Figure 2.7 is part of a client satisfaction survey from an evaluation study of the Arizona Welfare Reform Program.

Researchers in implementation studies sometimes use worker surveys or questionnaires to gather systematic data on worker knowledge, opinions, and recommendations about a program or services. Data from worker surveys serve two major research goals. First, they provide direct information about how far the new program's policies, procedures, and ethos have penetrated the agency's workforce. This information may be important for worker training efforts. A second potential use of this information is to help understand why the program may not be operating as planned. Data about worker knowledge and acceptance of the new policies can potentially be used either quantitatively or qualitatively as another explanatory factor in modeling operational outcomes. Figure 2.8 is an example of a worker survey used in the evaluation of the Indiana Welfare Reform Demonstration.

Another use of surveys or questionnaires in implementation research is to gather information about basic program, service, and administrative factors across a larger number of offices or service providers than may be visited in person. Often these program questionnaires are sent to respondents in advance and administered over the telephone. Telephone questionnaires can be an efficient means of collecting comparable descriptive information for a large group of program sites and may also include some questions about program managers' opinions and recommendations.

Designing surveys. There is a vast literature on survey design; it is beyond the scope of this book to review or summarize it.[18] This section suggests some guidelines for maximizing the reliability of survey data. Reliability refers to the degree to which respondents interpret questions as intended, and the degree to which their answers are interpreted by

text continued on page 69

Figure 2.6. *Survey about Program Exit Decisions*

3. I would like to read a list of reasons other people have given for deciding not to complete the process of being recertified for cash assistance. Please listen to each statement, and tell me whether any of these reasons affected your decision.

After I read the statement, please tell me whether this was, for you,

- a very important reason why you did not complete the recertification process,
- a somewhat important reason why you did not complete the process, or
- something that had nothing to do with why you did not complete the process.

	Very important	Somewhat important	Unrelated
A. DES asked me to provide a number of documents, and ...			
1) I was not able to provide them.	1	2	3
2) I was not willing to provide them.	1	2	3
B. I thought that the amount of my household's cash assistance would be reduced.	1	2	3
C. Because the amount of cash assistance we would have received was very small, it wasn't worth the trouble of going through the recertification process.	1	2	3
D. I thought that we might have to return money to DES from past overpayments of cash assistance.	1	2	3
E. I did not understand the changes in program rules and procedures	1	2	3

(F.–N.)

O. Were you aware that people can lose benefits if they do not cooperate with the child support enforcement office?
YES (ASK 1)   1
NO (GO TO Q. 4)   2

Source: Extract from an unpublished survey instrument used in Abt Associates' evaluation of the Arizona EMPOWER program.

Figure 2.7. *Client Satisfaction Survey*

C.1 INTERVIEWER: READ STATEMENT AND ASK, "Do you agree strongly, agree somewhat, neither agree nor disagree, disagree somewhat, or disagree strongly?" REMIND RESPONDENT OF CATEGORIES EVERY FEW STATEMENTS, OR AS NEEDED.

	Agree Strongly	Agree Somewhat	Neither Agree nor Disagree	Disagree Somewhat	Disagree Strongly	Don't Know
a. The DES office was open at convenient hours.	1	2	3	4	5	8
b. The DES office was in a convenient location.	1	2	3	4	5	8
c. You did not have to wait too long to see someone at DES.	1	2	3	4	5	8

C.2 ......

C.3 ......

C.4 These next questions ask more about your impressions of the DES office and how you were treated. Again, please think about your experiences during the process of applying for the cash assistance that you received in (DATE).

AFTER READING EACH STATEMENT, ASK: "Do you agree strongly, agree somewhat, neither agree nor disagree, disagree somewhat, or disagree strongly?"

	Agree Strongly	Agree Somewhat	Neither Agree nor Disagree	Disagree Somewhat	Disagree Strongly	Don't Know
a. In general, the eligibility interviewers and other staff at DES were courteous and polite to you.	1	2	3	4	5	8
b. The staff was knowledgeable about the cash assistance rules.	1	2	3	4	5	8

Source: Extract from an unpublished survey instrument used in Abt Associates' evaluation of the Arizona EMPOWER program.

Figure 2.8. *Welfare Agency Worker Survey*

Indiana Welfare Reform:
Implementation and Process Study
Survey of Family Case Coordinators
Fall 1999

10. When do you typically meet with a TANF client for the *first* time? *(Check one)*

_____ *at* the initial eligibility determination interview
_____ *after* the initial eligibility determination interview
_____ other (please specify):_____

11. Please rank the following eight policies in order of how much you emphasize each when you first meet with a TANF client. *(1 = Emphasize most strongly, 8 = Emphasize the least.)*

_____ A. the time limit
_____ B. the family cap
_____ C. the importance of seeking and obtaining a job
_____ D. availability of transitional benefits and other supportive services
_____ E. sanction penalties for noncompliance with IMPACT rules
_____ F. school attendance requirement
_____ G. immunization requirement
_____ H. the zero grant

12. In general, what advice do you currently give TANF clients about applying for jobs? *(Check one)*

_____ Apply for any job
_____ Apply only for higher-paying jobs
_____ Do not advise
_____ Other (please specify):_____

Source: Extract from an unpublished survey instrument used in Abt Associates' evaluation of Indiana's Welfare Reform program.

researchers as intended. In other words, are survey participants responding to the specific questions the study wants to ask and are researchers understanding the answers as intended? These issues are particularly important in a survey, as researchers do not usually have the opportunity to probe or ask respondents what they mean or to explain their answers.

Although no survey can guarantee that respondents will always interpret all questions in the same way, there are some strategies survey designers use to improve the reliability of responses.[19] For example, questions should avoid vague language. One example of a vaguely worded question is "How many of the people in your family are currently employed?" The term "family" is imprecise, and may mean different things to different people. A less ambiguous question would specify the types of individuals to be included in the particular application of the term "family." An example of a question that is vague in a different way is "Do you favor gun control legislation?" (Fowler 1984, 81). This question is not vague because of the terms it uses, but because it does not distinguish among a wide range of proposed gun control measures; a "yes" answer would be difficult to interpret. This question is not specific enough for its responses to add much to our knowledge of how people really feel along a broad spectrum of opinions.

Another way to increase reliability of survey responses is to narrow possible responses so that they are more likely to express the same intended meaning across all respondents. Fowler (1984, 83) presents an example of a poorly worded question that can elicit responses that are not comparable: "Why did you vote for Candidate A?" This question allows for too many different kinds of answers, such as "I liked the candidate's personality," "I liked the candidate's policies," "I have always voted Democratic," or "I thought Candidate B particularly weak." A more precise approach would be to narrow the type of consideration you are looking for, as in "Which of Candidate A's policies are attractive?" or "What most attracted you about Candidate A?" or "Why do you prefer Candidate A to Candidate B?" By being more specific in the wording of the question, the survey is more likely to elicit comparable answers from respondents.

Another technique in improving the reliability of responses is to avoid qualitative response categories wherever possible. An example of qualitative response categories is: "How often do you do X—always, frequently, often, sometimes, rarely, or never?" Although it may be easy to distinguish between "always" and "never," it is difficult to know clearly each respondent's way of distinguishing between "frequently" and "often." A far better approach would be to allow for alternative answers in terms of the frequency of X in a given time period, such as: "How often do you do X in a week?" Sometimes qualitative responses are desirable, however, as when the survey asks for a respondent's opinion of a given service. In these instances, the response choices should be few and easy to distinguish. The choices "excellent, very good, good, fair, poor, bad" tend to overlap and may mean different things to different respondents. A better way to approach the response categories would be to use fewer choices, such as "good, fair, poor," or to use a small range (usually 1 to 3 or 1 to 5) of numerical alternatives.

Survey sampling. As mentioned above, a reason to field a survey is to collect information that can be used to make statistical generalizations about some item of interest, such as program outcomes, program participation, client characteristics, or client satisfaction. Because client surveys in particular can be relatively expensive to mount, most studies using surveys select a sample of the group of interest in order to conserve resources. An important consideration for any survey is therefore how large a sample to select.

In most cases, the primary decision to make in determining sample size is how close to the true number, proportion, or size of the measured characteristic or value do you need your estimate based on the sample to be? In the language of political polling, how large a "margin of error," or how many "points plus or minus," can we tolerate in our sample estimate? Naturally, there is no hard and fast rule about how precise an estimate based on a sample should be. The question of how much error we can live with in a sample estimate has to do with the importance of the information sought and the risks involved in the decisions based on the sample estimate. For example, the standards of precision used to calculate the risks of using a new medical intervention on children ought to be a lot higher than the standards used to predict the portion of the population that will purchase a new breakfast cereal.

The question of sample size is further complicated by other issues. For example, a study rarely uses a survey to measure only one thing in the population of interest. Because precision in the sample estimate is based in part on the prevalence of a given characteristic or feature being measured, researchers may need to decide which measures are more important, or may simply base sampling strategy on the measure that requires the largest sample for a given level of precision. Table 2.2 presents a quick guide to sample size requirements for various levels of precision. The figures in the table indicate the number of percentage points

Table 2.2. *Levels of Precision for Survey Samples: Half Width of Confidence Interval*

| Sample size | *Percentage of sample with/without given characteristic* | | | | |
	5/95	*10/90*	*20/80*	*30/70*	*50/50*
50	±6	±8	±11	±13	±14
100	4	6	8	9	10
200	3	4	6	6	7
500	2	3	4	4	4
1000	1	2	3	3	3

Source: Fowler (1984, 42).

Notes: Chances are 95 in a 100 that the real proportion of a given measure in the general population is plus or minus the percentage points indicated in the appropriate cell. Assume simple random sampling.

"plus or minus" the true proportion of a given characteristic at the 95 percent confidence level. That is, chances are 95 out of a 100 that the true proportion is plus or minus the sample estimate by the number of percentage points indicated in the table.

A second potential issue in determining sample size is the importance of subsamples. For example, if researchers want to know something about a particular group among the target population (the "sampling frame"), the study may have to sample disproportionately, to observe enough individuals in the subgroup to make reliable estimates about their characteristics. For example, if a study wants to know more details about ex-TANF families that have missed a meal in the past week, and these families represent 20 percent of the total population of ex-TANF families, the sample would have to be increased by a factor of five to achieve the same precision in estimates about the subgroup as for the population as a whole. If the particular group can be identified before the survey interview, the sample could be "stratified," or divided into different groups, with proportionally more people sampled out of the strata of interest.

Determining sample sizes for surveys can be complicated by a variety of factors related to the characteristics of the groups of interest in the study. In general, a good rule of thumb in social science research is to accept estimates that have a 95 percent chance of being within 5 percentage points plus or minus the true value in the population. As table 2.2 shows, samples of 400 to 500 would ordinarily suffice to meet this standard.

Response rates and nonresponse bias. Another important consideration in assessing sample sizes is the response rate, or the percentage of
individuals who can be located and who complete the survey. No survey
can expect to have 100 percent of its survey sample complete an interview
questionnaire, whatever the survey "mode," or method of respondent
contact. The solution to less than perfect response rates seems simple. If
the response rate is 50 percent, simply sample twice as many individuals
for the survey as needed for the count of completed surveys.

The problem with the simple solution to survey nonresponse is that
people who complete the survey may be different from those who do not.
For example, if the survey is a telephone survey, the people who are not
located may not have a telephone or stable residence. Individuals who
are located but who refuse to be interviewed may be likely to have had
more negative experiences in the TANF program, or may be more dis-
trustful of research on government programs. In either case, the people
who do answer the survey questionnaire are likely to be systematically
different from those who do not, thereby biasing the survey results away
from the true population measures.

Because of the problem of nonresponse bias, social scientists have
loosely established standards for response rates, just as there are loosely
established standards for statistical precision in sampling strategies. For
example, results from surveys with response rates above 80 percent are
considered to be reliable, while results from surveys with response rates
below 60 percent are often viewed with suspicion. Note again that there
are no hard and fast rules for response rates. Moreover, if something is
known about the differences in characteristics between those that
responded and those that did not, statistical methods may be used to measure potential bias, or at least to indicate the likely direction of the bias.
The magnitude of the nonresponse bias increases with the size of the true
difference between responders and nonresponders.

Survey Modes. There are three major survey modes: mail, telephone,
and in-person. Because the major expense of a survey is labor time (both
for interviewing and locating respondents), mail surveys are generally the
least expensive to mount, with in-person surveys being the most expensive.
Response rates usually rank in reverse order, with mail surveys yielding the
lowest rates and in-person surveys the best. Because mail surveys generally
yield low response rates (rarely higher than 50 percent), client surveys are
often "mixed mode" surveys, with a majority of interviews completed by
telephone, with some portion of the nonresponders contacted in person.

Sometimes in an effort to economize, implementation studies will attempt to "piggyback" client surveys on some program activity, most notably the eligibility or redetermination interview. Workers in selected offices during selected periods will be asked to give clients the opportunity to fill out a questionnaire while completing those activities. Naturally, this approach will only work if applicants or clients being redetermined are the target population for the study or for the group of research questions addressed in the survey. Moreover, respondents may not focus well on the survey in the middle of all the other paper work and reading that is often required for the application or redetermination interview. Nevertheless, this approach is convenient, inexpensive, and is likely to yield high response rates, particularly if the questionnaire focuses on a small number of questions and takes little time to complete.

Although mail surveys are usually not recommended for clients because of low response rates, they can work well with worker or manager questionnaires. A common approach for worker surveys is to distribute them at the TANF office or service provider site and to ask workers to complete them and leave them in sealed envelopes in a secure location or lock box on the site.

Ethnographic Research and Data Collection

A final important data collection strategy sometimes used in implementation studies is ethnographic research. "Ethnography" has no one accepted meaning or application in social science.[20] In general, it refers to research that analyzes the meaning and significance of social practices or norms. In recent years, ethnographic research methods and approaches have gained some currency in evaluation research. In part, this is because policymakers have realized that in order to understand stakeholders' (both clients and workers) behavioral responses to changes in policy, services, or programs, it is useful to know what those changes mean in the context of the stakeholders' ongoing social and cultural milieu.

Using the term "ethnography" in a generic sense (meaning research about how individuals deal with changes in their social and cultural environment) rather than in a technical sense (meaning the way in which professional anthropologists may prefer to use the term), one example of its use in implementation research is the "street-level bureaucracy" approach to studying program operations and policy implementation.[21] At its extreme, the theory of street-level bureaucracy is that policy is made from the "bottom up" by the way it is interpreted and put in practice by service-delivery-level workers. In some instances, the actual implementation of policy may bear little resemblance to the spirit or letter of the regulations developed in Washington, D.C., or in state capitals. Even for those who do not accept the more extreme view of the theory, the fact that in practice, public policy "is" what happens in the interchange between bureaucracies and clients is a powerful insight. Research in street-level bureaucracy thus focuses on the content, quality, and meaning of that interchange in understanding how policy gets implemented.

Another type of ethnographic research sometimes conducted in implementation studies focuses on the interaction between social programs and policies and the daily lives of those affected by those programs and policies. In this approach, researchers try to understand client behavior in the face of new policies as it relates to their other concerns, activities, aspirations, and beliefs.[22] Here, the focus is on first-person accounts by clients of how changes in program policies or services are integrated into the daily context of their lives and their families' lives.

There are two basic data collection methods connected with ethnographic research. One is intensive and extended interviewing. In this approach, the researcher engages informants in more casual, unstructured multiple conversations in an attempt to gain their confidence and understand their concerns, beliefs, and values often over a long period of time.

Another data collection methodology related to ethnography is "participant observation." In this approach, researchers remain at a site or neighborhood for extended periods of time to become (as much as possible) members of the society or culture they are studying. In this sense, ethnographers attempt to understand the target group's way of life from first-hand experience and extended observations.

Linking Data Sources and Collection Strategies with Research Questions

The ultimate choice of data sources and data collection should begin with the information needed to answer the set of research questions addressed by an implementation study. The previous chapter closed with a listing of a selected group of specific research questions that may be included in a comprehensive implementation study. Table 2.3 links the questions with the potential data sources and data collection strategies discussed in this chapter.

Table 2.3. *Research Questions, Data Sources, and Data Collection Strategies*

Research domain and questions	Data sources/collection strategies
Theoretical and practical basis	
How was the program planned and developed?	Program planning documents, minutes of planning meetings
	Open-ended interviews with state- and local-level TANF program management and staff, other relevant agency management and staff, and informants from executive and legislative branches
What general and specific goals is the program designed to meet? Are they feasible?	Program documents, legislative material, public information materials, and newspaper articles
	Open-ended interviews with state- and local-level TANF program management and staff, other relevant agency management and staff, informants from executive and legislative branches, and public interest and advocacy groups
How are the program's prescribed policies, procedures, activities, and services designed to advance the program's general and specific goals?	Program planning documents, worker policy and procedure manuals
	Open-ended interviews with state- and local-level TANF program management and staff, other relevant agency management and staff, and public interest and advocacy groups
Program environment	
What are the demographic, social, cultural, political, and economic environments in which the program operates?	Background statistical data, including local and regional economic and demographic conditions and trends; program planning documents; relevant research reports and journalistic accounts
	Open-ended interviews and focus groups with state- and local-level TANF program management and staff, other relevant agency management and staff, informants from executive and legislative branches, public interest and advocacy groups, and clients
	Ethnographic research
In what ways has the program's environment affected its implementation, operations, and results?	Open-ended interviews and focus groups with state- and local-level TANF program management and staff, other relevant agency management and staff, informants from executive and legislative branches, public interest and advocacy groups, and clients
	Ethnographic research

(*continued*)

Table 2.3. *Continued*

Research domain and questions	Data sources/collection strategies
Are the necessary resources to operate the program "in place"?	
Are all required resources available?	Open-ended interviews and focus groups with state- and local-level TANF program management and staff, other relevant agency management and staff, informants from executive and legislative branches, public interest and advocacy groups, and clients Management reports Structured observations
Which resources are in short supply and why? How does this vary by locality?	Open-ended interviews and focus groups with state- and local-level TANF program management and staff, other relevant agency management and staff, informants from executive and legislative branches, public interest and advocacy groups, and clients Management reports Structured observations
What implications does the level of resources have for program operations and performance?	Open-ended interviews and focus groups with state- and local-level TANF program management and staff, other relevant agency management and staff, informants from executive and legislative branches, public interest and advocacy groups, clients
Are program processes and systems operating as planned?	
Are all program processes and systems operating as planned?	Open-ended interviews and focus groups with state- and local-level TANF program management and staff, and clients Structured observations Administrative data
How and why are various program processes and systems not operating as planned? Does this vary by locality? What are the implications for program operations and performance and client outcomes? How may program processes and systems be improved?	Open-ended interviews and focus groups with state- and local-level TANF program management and staff, other agency management and staff, service providers, advocacy groups, and clients Worker surveys, client surveys Structured observations

(continued)

Table 2.3. *Continued*

Research domain and questions	Data sources/collection strategies
Is the program reaching the intended target population?	
How many clients are scheduled for various program activities and services? What proportion of clients scheduled for program activities and services attend as scheduled? What other services are clients using?	Open-ended interviews and focus groups with state- and local-level TANF program management and staff, other agency management and staff, and service providers Worker surveys Structured observations Administrative data Management reports
What are the content and quality of program activities and services? Are the content and quality sufficient to meet program expectations? If not, how and why?	(same as above)
What are the implications of the content, timing, and quality of services for program operations and performance? How does this vary by locality? How may services be improved?	(same as above)
Is the program achieving desired outcomes?	

What are the relevant outcomes of program clients? What are the changes in their overall well-being?	Administrative data
	    TANF administrative systems
	    Quarterly wage data
	    Service provider data
	Surveys and focus groups of clients and ex-clients
	Ethnographic studies

NOTES

1. Even in the age of computers, most state welfare agencies still maintain hard-copy files of program events and transactions, even if only as legal documentation.

2. Note that hard-copy files are not always complete or well organized; re-creating a program history on their basis can be a labor-intensive and risky prospect.

3. Recently, and in large part due to the introduction of time-limited eligibility, states have either been developing administrative systems with the capacity to maintain such historical records of program participation or are using monthly file abstracts to create summary program histories (for example, whether or not a case was active, and/or the amount of benefits received monthly) for each client and/or case.

4. Another data collection method commonly used to collect nonprogram information about individuals and families is surveys; see page 61.

5. The quarterly wage system includes information on earnings reported by employers.

6. Nonwelfare state-level administrative systems commonly used in research on welfare reform are the quarterly wage reporting system, the child support enforcement system, and the child welfare system.

7. This is not always the case, as jobs "off the books," casual employment, and self-employment are usually not included in the quarterly wage system. However, when an individual's gross income is of interest, the quarterly wage system is probably more accurate than client recollection. Moreover, the quarterly wage system provides data about earnings over a standardized period of time and in a comparable way for multiple individuals.

8. An important exception is studies in which the potential disparity between two or more data sources is an important point of the study. For example, a topic of interest to welfare administrators and policymakers is the degree to which client reports of earnings and employer reports of earnings do not match (and why).

9. That is, unless, of course, the purpose of the study is to compare the answers from those two sources.

10. Note that the issue of data sources for some research questions may not be resolved until some preliminary research is conducted.

11. For an excellent and detailed summary of the issues involved in organizing and conducting fieldwork for research on social programs, see Nightingale and Rossman (1994). Note that although focus groups are sometimes conducted in conjunction with site visits, this book treats focus groups separately from other on-site data collection activities.

12. For example, in some states, clients that are undergoing psychological counseling or are being treated for child neglect may not be technically exempt from participation, but may have their counseling or treatment counted as participation. Some informants may not consider this policy an exemption and may not include it as part of their answer.

13. Some newer automated systems include case narratives.

14. Note that with either approach, an implementation study that seeks to recreate a longitudinal record of TANF families would need to collect "snapshots" of the administrative system at multiple time points. Usually, because most TANF agencies archive administrative data (usually a shortened version of client records) on a monthly basis, copies of the administrative records are made at that time.

15. Note that focus groups are also used in program or service design to learn more about potential client needs and likely reactions to developing policies. Here we only consider the use of focus groups for implementation research.

16. For an excellent detailed account of how to organize and run focus groups, see Krueger (1988). Also see Dean (1994).

17. This is not entirely correct, of course. As discussed earlier in this chapter, overlapping administrative systems may include some relevant information about ex-TANF recipients.

18. See, for example, the text and bibliography in Fowler (1984) and Miller (1994).

19. The following text borrows heavily from both Fowler (1984) and Miller (1994).

20. For a convenient summary of ethnography and its use in applied social research, see Atkinson and Hammersley (1994). Also see the papers by Edin (2003) and Brodkin (2003).

21. The *locus classicus* for the street-level bureaucracy approach is Lipsky (1980). See also, for example, Brodkin (1997).

22. See, for example, Edin and Lein (1997).

3

Documenting Implementation

The previous chapter surveyed the wide range of data and data collection strategies needed to address the variety of questions that may be posed in an implementation study. This chapter discusses how to use the data collected to develop descriptive accounts of how the program is implemented, using welfare reform as our example.

A central goal of most implementation research is to "tell the story" of the program—to answer the question "What is happening?" in a comprehensive way. For convenience, this question may be thought of as having two main components: a nonquantitative component and a quantitative component. The first part may be called the "program narrative," and the second part may be called "descriptive statistics." Although we discuss each set of analyses separately in this chapter, complete descriptions of a program's implementation usually include both parts.[1]

An important aspect of documenting implementation also focuses on the perspectives of those affected by the program—"How do stakeholders perceive and experience the program?" In these analyses, the views of policymakers, program planners, managers, workers, and participating families are fleshed out from the evidence of surveys, in-depth interviews, observations, focus groups, and ethnographic research. Although stakeholder perspectives may reflect imperfect knowledge, personal biases, and subjective views of reality, they can be useful in understanding why a program operates as it does and why it produces the results it does.

This chapter includes five sections: organizing data for the program narrative, preparing the program narrative, using graphic presentations, using descriptive statistics, and reporting stakeholder perspectives. The chapter concludes with a table presenting the descriptive analysis strategies to be used to address the illustrative research questions listed at the end of chapters 1 and 2.

Organizing Data for the Program Narrative

Program narratives—discursive descriptions of how a program operates—are probably the most familiar products of implementation research. They often set the stage for the other aspects of implementation research, including, for example, whether the program is operating as planned and why it is operating as it is. The program narrative helps anchor the evaluative and explanatory functions of implementation research in a concrete framework. A major challenge of constructing the program narrative is building a coherent account from the many open-ended interviews, program observations, and program documents used to collect data.

A convenient first step in building the "story" of the program is synthesizing the varied accounts of the program collected through interviews and on-site observations. The interview guides used for on-site data collection already include an organized format for the synthesis. Recall that the guides were initially developed on the basis of a preliminary model of the program.

As discussed in chapter 1, each of these topics potentially includes many specific research questions. The interview guides were developed by selecting the appropriate specific questions for each type of informant. After on-site data collection has been completed, and if informants were correctly identified and able to address all or most of the specific research questions, the interview guides with responses should contain much of the raw data needed to develop coherent and comprehensive program narratives.

To create successful program narratives, informants' responses need to be combined in two basic ways. First, the accounts must be combined across topics. It is unlikely that any one informant will have provided comprehensive descriptions of the entire program and its results. The story of the program—from program planning through development and start-up, as well as ongoing operations and outcomes—needs to be built up from partial views of the whole.

A second, and sometimes more problematic, descriptive synthesis begins with multiple accounts of the same aspects of the program. Occasionally, informants' descriptions of the same policies, procedures, or services do not agree. In some instances, disagreement is expected. For example, where discretion is allowed at the worker, supervisory, or local office level, variation is expected across those individuals or administrative entities. The complete program narrative will attempt to document those differences and their relative prevalence.

Although differing accounts across informants may be perfectly normal, they may also indicate the presence of eccentric views or opinions, as well as miscommunications between informant and researcher or misinterpretation by the researcher. It is also possible that the informant is simply mistaken. Part of synthesizing accounts across multiple informants and across multiple researchers includes discriminating among eccentric, incorrect, and poorly communicated responses.

First Steps: Combining Multiple Accounts

A first step in organizing qualitative descriptions to create a narrative synthesis involves individual site researchers and their data. A convenient way to organize and summarize data collected from open-ended interviews is to combine responses to the same questions from different interview guides. (Researchers who use word processing on site have a distinct advantage in this stage of analysis.) This process begins by grouping all the varied responses to a particular question together in a single interview guide, indicating the source for each response. An example from a study of subsidized child care programs is presented in figure 3.1.

The second step in combining multiple accounts is to review the responses to each question or topic for consistency. Responses that agree may be grouped together. At this point in synthesizing descriptive data from an individual researcher's notes, it may be convenient to check for consistency both within and across research sites. How varied are responses to each interview question or topic? Do the variations seem to group by research site or by type of respondent? Do they exist within sites and across similar types of respondents? Are the variations expected on the basis of prior knowledge or are they a surprise?

Figure 3.1. *Synthesizing Responses to an Open-Ended Interview*

5.D.1—What types of automated systems are used in operating subsidized child care programs?

In *State A*, there is a state automated system that has two main parts—one is an automated reimbursement system, and the other is a system containing information about subsidy families. Before 1996, the state used a paper system. In April 1996, the DCD computerized this system and now everyone seems happier. The main problem now is that most of the counties are not networked together nor linked directly to the state system, so information still must be sent to the state and downloaded into the state database. This problem is common within many government agencies, but the DHHS has selected DCD to be part of an Interface Pilot Project to help remedy this problem (*State CC Director*).

Local purchasing agencies are required to keep several pieces of information on the families and providers participating in the child care subsidy system. These data are entered on the local level and then downloaded into the state system on a regular basis. The data tend to be very reliable, although there are often compatibility issues and data must be processed twice (i.e., once for the local database and once for the state database). This makes the process very time consuming and burdensome. The Interface Pilot Project should help this process as well (*State CC Director*).

Blue County's automated system for SCC administration was created for JC DSS by the state and thus is compatible with the system used by the DCD. The main problem with the JC SCC program's automated system is its data concerning TANF status. The automated system created to run the Work First program is not compatible with the subsidy automated system and, whenever a TANF family's Work First status changes, the Work First case worker must notify the child care worker assigned to that case and have this person ensure that the data is updated in the subsidy system. This leaves a lot of room for error. Since subsidy policies are the same for TANF and non-TANF families, this does not cause problems for subsidy program operations. However, it can affect which pot of money is used to fund a family's subsidies and it makes long range planning more difficult (*Blue County DSS Supervisor*).

(*continued*)

Figure 3.1. *Continued*

> In *Green County,* the computerized reimbursement system is different
> from, and more detailed than, the state's. For example, the county's
> system (purchased from a computer system vendor in 1994) includes
> microdata on participating families taken from the application form and
> from patterns of subsidy use. A programmer has been trying (unsuc-
> cessfully) to interface the county's system with the state's administrative
> system (*Green County DSS Director*).
>
> In *Orange County,* CCRI maintains its own computerized system that
> tracks use of subsidies and payments to providers. This system is also
> incompatible with the state's (*Orange County CCRI staff*).

Source: Unpublished interview notes from Abt Associates' National Study of Child Care for Low-Income Families.

The next step in synthesizing responses from individual researchers' interview guides is to group topics by those that show no important variations, those that appear to vary in expected ways, and those that vary in unexpected ways. For responses that show no important variations, a summary statement of their content should be developed. For responses that vary in expected ways, a set of summary statements for each type of response should be developed, and the relative prevalence of each variation across respondents and sites should be indicated. Finally, those responses to purely descriptive questions that reveal unexpected inconsistencies or disagreements should be highlighted for potential calls back to sites, or for resolution by other more reliable respondents or documents.

At the end of the process of combining multiple accounts by respondents, each site researcher should have a comprehensive summary of the variety of answers (or one consistent answer) to each question or topic in the interview guides. The summary should indicate the source or sources for each response, as well as whether the responses vary as expected or are contradictory. Note that because the interview guides were designed on the basis of a provisional understanding of the program and its components, this first level of descriptive synthesis begins to flesh out the details of the provisional model and the degree to which it accurately represents "what is happening."

Next Steps: Synthesizing Data across Researchers

A natural next step in creating a narrative description is to combine the interview guides into a single guide summarizing the findings of multiple researchers. One convenient way to synthesize qualitative data across researchers is to bring site researchers together for a meeting to share and discuss findings from the field.[2]

The most direct way to organize the meeting is by major topic areas covered in the interviews and observations. For example, for the topic area covering local TANF office approaches to TANF applicant and client orientations, each site researcher describes how these activities happen in the offices they visited. The meeting moderator summarizes individual researcher findings on a large flip chart, including the major points of the group discussion. The group then determines the highlights for this topic area. This technique gives an efficient overview of what is similar or not across research sites. The topic discussions can also uncover further inconsistent or contradictory findings that may require researchers to recontact their informants.

Bringing researchers together after fieldwork is also a convenient time to question the overall approach to the implementation study. Often, field research can uncover shortcomings in a research plan, particularly in the choice of informants and research sites. For example, in a study of welfare reform in Arizona, the initial research plan did not include visits to local Department of Employment Security (DES) offices, where TANF clients are assessed and assigned to job search and/or other employment-related services. Researchers initially assumed that the informants could provide some descriptive information about what happens at Employment Security offices. In fact, although caseworkers routinely referred TANF clients to DES, the workers had no idea of what happened there. Each field researcher on the project met with the same lack of knowledge from TANF caseworkers. This finding was, of course, interesting in itself, revealing the little contact between the welfare office and the agency delivering employment services to welfare clients.[3] It also showed that the initial research plan was inadequate, and so in subsequent rounds of field research for this project, some DES offices were visited.

If the meeting of field researchers is successful, it will further flesh out the narrative's skeletal structure. In fact, the notes taken during the researchers' meeting often are used directly by the report authors to structure relevant sections of the report. Those notes should indicate the major "story lines" of how various parts of a program operate, as well the variations in approaches found in the field.

Preparing the Program Narrative

After highlighting the major findings about program structure and operations from interview guides and other qualitative data collection activities, the facts need to be woven together into a coherent story. Rarely is this as straightforward a task as it may seem when reading a skillfully composed program description; the challenges are many. For example, what level of detail should be carried over from the raw data into the text? How should the narrative be ordered? How should similarities and differences among program sites be handled? There are, in fact, no hard and fast answers to these questions. The final choices are a combination of stylistic preferences, the specific focus of the research, and the nature and richness of the raw data. We present here a few options that may help researchers make these choices.

Level of Detail

The question of what level of detail is needed in a program narrative can sometimes appear intractable. For example, when describing a program activity, such as a job club training session, should the study report the content of each topic or simply summarize the issues covered? When describing the program application process, should the study include descriptions of the room or carrel used for eligibility interviews or simply state that the interview took place in a carrel or a room? What level is detail is desirable or necessary?

The short answer to the last question is to include the level of detail needed to support program assessment and explanation. For example, if the research design includes questions only about the *content* of job club training, a course syllabus may be sufficient evidence to show what topics are included. On the other hand, if the study promises to judge the *quality* of job club training, some details about how well the topics are presented and delivered will be needed to support the analysis.

Even when the level of detail is clearly directed by the research questions and analysis objectives, the issue of where to place details and how many details to include may be stylistic. Some details may be put in appendices or selectively included only to illustrate a point or to provide data for a specific conclusion or observation. In the end, factual details should serve the "program's story" and not simply list endless facts because they happened to be met in the course of data collection.

Ordering the Narrative

There are many different ways to order a program narrative in an implementation study. The optimal choice depends on a number of factors, including the structure of the program, the degree of comparability and standardization across program sites, the special focus of the study, and its major research questions. The following examples are some ways to organize narrative description:[4]

- *Conceptual model.* For a comprehensive description of a program from its theoretical basis to its outcomes, it may be most convenient to follow the logic of a program's conceptual (or "logic") model when describing its implementation. The logic model explains the hypothetical causal relationships between the program intervention and its intended outcomes. The simplest form of a program's logic model usually includes a description of the specific problem or issue the program is designed to deal with, the program context, the target population, program "inputs" (services, benefits, and activities), and short- and long-term outcomes. This approach often works well as it simplifies combining description and evaluation ("Does the implemented program mirror the conceptual model?").
- *Client flow.* In this approach, the description follows the path of a program participant from application to program exit. Because the narrative mirrors an idealized "path" through a program, this approach is often used to describe welfare-to-work demonstration programs. It is less successful when applied to programs that do not have "linear" participation patterns where one activity or outcome clearly follows another in a single path, or when applied to programs that may have multiple participation paths or patterns.
- *Chronological order.* Presenting the program narrative in chronological order may be most appropriate for a formative evaluation or for a study that describes and analyzes program design and start-up experiences.

- *"Programmatic" areas.* This variant of the client flow model may work well when participation patterns and client experiences vary widely within each program activity or service. In this instance, when the "client flow" breaks down into multiple "flows," it may be easier to organize description by topic area—such as eligibility determination, assessment, work-related activities, support services, job finding services, job retention services, and counseling.

Using Graphic Presentations

Graphic presentations are very useful in summarizing descriptions of program models. Tables or figures can present the "whole" program in one view and give a dynamic quality to otherwise static narratives. Graphic presentations work particularly well with three types of program narratives: the conceptual program model, the client flow model, and the model of programmatic areas. Examples of each are presented below, including two examples of a client flow model using somewhat different approaches.

Figure 3.2 is an illustration of a conceptual model of a volunteer community project for young adults. The first column indicates the program's activities and resources, and the arrows connect the activities to their intended short-term and long-term outcomes.

Using a graphical illustration of the client flow in a program can be particularly helpful in portraying the relationship among the various steps and possible decisions and outcomes in a program. Figure 3.3 is an example of a client flow model from an evaluation of a welfare reform program in Florida. The figure shows the steps involved in the process that Florida uses to review cases that are soon to reach time limits on TANF assistance.

Using Tables to Present Variations across Research Sites

Programs with a great deal of variation across states, local offices, or program service sites can be a challenge to describe in purely narrative form. Reports filled with long series of paragraphs each describing a specific aspect of program operations in a different site are likely to be confusing and a chore for readers to plow through. Tables summarizing variations across program sites can often communicate the range of program approaches and experiences more effectively and efficiently than narration.

Figure 3.2. *Conceptual Program Model*

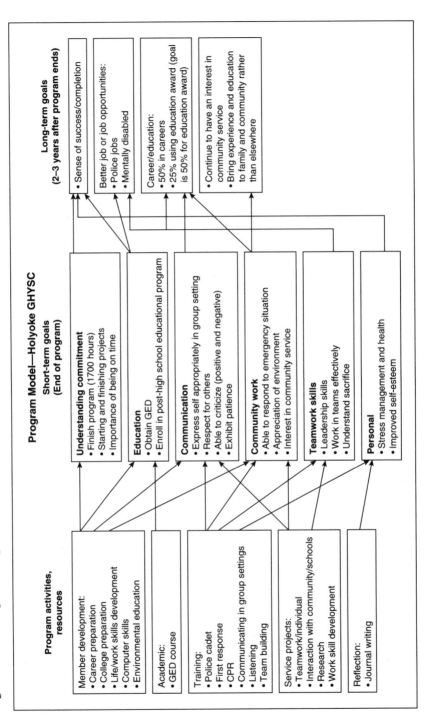

Source: Abt Associates, Inc. (2001).

Figure 3.3. *Client Flow Model*

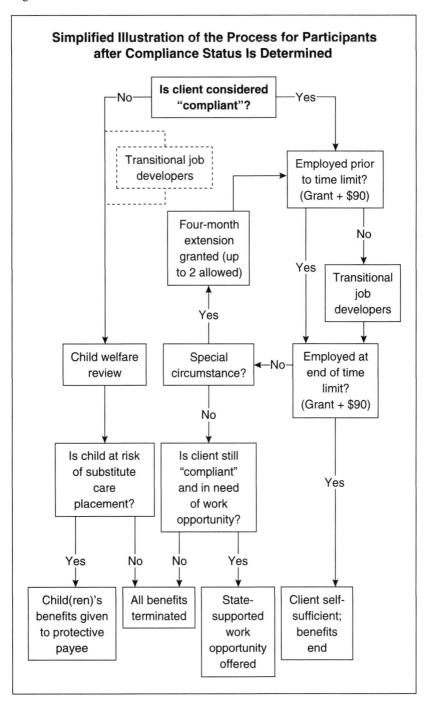

Simplified Illustration of the Process for Participants after Compliance Status Is Determined

Source: Bloom et al. (1999, 16–17).

Multisite implementation studies usually use two forms of descriptive tables, depending on the type and level of variation depicted. For example, if a study wants to present variation across sites in the presence of specific policies, activities, or services, the most direct approach is to use a table that creates cells for each policy or service for each program site. Table 3.1, taken from an implementation study of the Job Opportunity and Basic Skills (JOBS) Program, illustrates this approach.

Sometimes, the particular focus of a descriptive section is on variations within given policies, activities, services, or some other program feature. For these tables, each cell includes a short phrase or sentence describing the specific variation in that program feature present in a given site. Table 3.2, taken from the same series of reports on the implementation of JOBS, illustrates this approach.

Using Descriptive Statistics

Many aspects of "what is happening" in a program are best characterized using statistical data. In particular, measurements of group phenomena—

Table 3.1. *Variation in Presence of Program Features by State*

JOBS Services and Activities Selected by States		
State	*Elective*	*Optional*
Maryland	Job search On-the-job training	Postsecondary education Alternative work experience Self-initiated education and training Other activities
Michigan	Job search On-the-job training Work supplementation CWEP	Self-initiated education and training
Mississippi	Job search On-the-job training	Postsecondary education Alternative work experience Self-initiated education and training Other activities

Source: Hagen and Lurie (1992, 63).

Table 3.2. *Variation in Content of Program Features by State*

		Content of Job Readiness Activities		
State	Site	*Most common content areas*		
Maryland	Baltimore	Interviewing skills	Job search	Life skills
	Anne Arundel	Interviewing skills	Job search	Life skills
	Dorchester	Interviewing skills	Job search	Life skills
Michigan	Wayne	Literacy	Life skills	Motivation
	Kalamazoo	Résumé preparation	Job search	Life skills
	Tuscola	Motivation	Decision-making	Personal appearance
Mississippi	Hinds	Personal appearance	Attitudes	Job search
	Harrison	(Varies with case manager)		
	Quitman	(No formal activities)		

Source: Hagen and Lurie (1993, 52).

such as client characteristics, participation patterns, client outcomes, and caseload change—are best described using numbers. In well-constructed implementation studies, statistical data are often woven into program narratives to express the scope and scale of project operations, as well as client experiences and outcomes. Basically, anything that may be expressed in numerical form may be tabulated and subjected to statistical analysis.

Before discussing the use of descriptive statistics in implementation research, some basic definitions and distinctions may be helpful. "Descriptive" statistics means the measurement of some set of variables across a population or groups within a population. The simplest form of descriptive statistics is often a list of characteristics and the frequency or mean of each characteristic in a given population, such as welfare recipients in a particular county or state. Also useful in implementation research are statistics that describe and compare important subpopulations. In the policy area of welfare reform, some important subgroups include, for example, two-parent welfare families, families with preschool children, and "child-only" cases.

More complex statistical analyses explore relationships between or among variables. Because these types of relational analyses are so often associated with hypotheses about what lies behind program experiences and results, they are not discussed until chapter 4.

Another important distinction to keep in mind is the distinction between the "universe" and a "sample." The universe is the entire population of the group being studied, such as a state's TANF caseload, for example. A sample is some smaller set of individuals taken from the universe. The distinction is important because while descriptive statistics for the universe describe that group with certainty, the description of a sample is representative of the universe within some confidence interval (see the discussion of sampling strategy in chapter 2). Similarly, when two universes are compared, the measured differences in characteristics are the real variance between the two groups. But when sample populations are compared, the apparent differences may not be statistically significant within an acceptable confidence interval.

A final basic distinction applies to the types of data used to describe program experiences. That is the distinction between cross-sectional and longitudinal data. Cross-sectional data describe something at a point in time (for example, the characteristics of program participants in a given month), or averaged over a given period (for example, the percentage of program participants entering employment in a given year). Longitudinal data describe change over time (for example, trends in monthly TANF caseloads, or trends in the percentage of TANF participants combining work with welfare).

The remainder of this section reviews a variety of quantitative analysis strategies for program descriptions, including statistical descriptions of client characteristics, program experiences and participation patterns, and program outcomes.

Client Characteristics

Along with the question "What is the program?" the question "Who is the program's clientele?" is among the most basic descriptive issues dealt with in implementation research on social programs. One way to answer the question is to refer to the program's target population and its eligibility rules. But a statistical description of client characteristics is an indispensable part of the answer to the question "What is happening?" and may lead to questions about whether the program is being implemented as planned.

The most common approach to analyzing client characteristics for descriptive purposes is a table with two columns—one column lists categories and individual variables and the second column indicates the relevant statistical data for each measure. Categorical variables (such as ethnic groups) are usually measured as percentages, while continuous variables (such as age of casehead) are often measured as means, or averages. Sometimes it is convenient to convert all measures to percentages by creating categories for continuous variables. Table 3.3 is an example of a straightforward approach to depicting client characteristics for a welfare reform program in Florida.[5]

An important question for descriptions of client characteristics concerns which characteristics to measure and present in the study. After all, there are almost an infinite number of facts about people that could be observed and analyzed. The simplest answer is that the variables used should have some strategic purpose related to the program and the research questions asked by the implementation study. For example, client characteristics related to the program's target population—such as the number of dependent children in a family— are of obvious interest and contribute to analyses of whether and to what degree the program is reaching its intended clientele. Similarly, characteristics linked to program rules or requirements—such as the age of the youngest child, or whether or not both parents are present in the household—may also be important descriptive variables for understanding and evaluating program operations and participation patterns.

Variables thought to be linked to a program's outcomes may also be important data for implementation research. Implementation studies of welfare reform programs often include information about client characteristics related to the probability of employment, such as educational attainment, prior employment history, and prior welfare experience. These data may be useful in analyses of whether and to what degree the appropriate services are provided to the right people. Table 3.3 illustrates this point well. For example, research has shown that the probability of future employment is higher for individuals with recent employment experience and higher educational attainment. Similarly, single parents with preschool children may experience difficulty in arranging for child care as a barrier to employment.

In the descriptive analysis of participation and outcomes, important subgroups are often compared for different patterns of program

Table 3.3. *Client Characteristics*

Florida's Family Transition Program—Selected Demographic Characteristics of the Report Sample at the Time of Random Assignment

Characteristic	Report sample
Gender (percent)	
Female	97.2
Male	2.9
Age (percent)	
Under 20 years	7.2
20–24 years	25.2
25–34 years	44.7
35–44 years	19.7
45 years and over	3.3
Average age (years)	29.1
Marital status (percent)	
Never married	49.4
Married, not living with spouse	24.4
Separated	4.8
Divorced	19.8
Other	1.7
Age of youngest child (percent)	
2 years and under	42.4
3–5 years	26.3
6 years and over	31.3
Ever worked (percent)	90.7
Highest degree/diploma earned (percent)	
GED	10.1
High school diploma	44.2
Technical/two-year college	5.5
Four-year (or more) college degree	0.9
None of the above	39.4

Source: Bloom et al. (1999, 16–17).

experiences and outcomes. Those comparisons may lead to hypotheses about important meaningful relationships among client characteristics and program participation and outcomes. Table 3.4 is an example of descriptive statistics that focuses on potential differences in key demographic and socioeconomic variables among important subgroups of clients in a study of Virginia's welfare reform program.

Table 3.4. *Comparative Statistics in a Description of Program Participants*

Comparison of Time Limit Cases, Other Closed Cases, and All VIEW Cases		
Time limit sample (n = 328)	*Closed case sample (n = 402)*	*VIEW mandatory cases (n = 3,249)*
Age (percent)		
Under 30 years	36	48	46
30 to 40 years	48	42	39
Over 40 years	16	11	15
Mean age (years)	33.9	31.3	31.8
Education level (percent)		
8th grade or less	8.2	8.5	9.6
9th grade to 11th grade	31.7	26.9	33.6
12th grade	36.9	37.8	41.1
GED	11.6	8.5	7.9
Any postsecondary	11.0	9.5	7.7
Data missing	0.6	9.0	0.0
Number of children in case (percent)		
1	33.2	48.0	39.0
2	32.0	36.1	32.9
3	23.9	10.2	17.7
4	10.9	5.0	9.9
Mean number of children	2.2	1.7	n.a.

Source: Gordon et al. (1999, 24).

Program Experiences and Participation Patterns

Describing the variety of program experiences and participation patterns using quantitative data is a common objective of implementation studies. There are a number of analytic and presentational options. A common way to classify descriptions of program experiences and participation patterns is by whether they are *cross-sectional* ("point-in-time" snapshots) or *longitudinal* (changes over time). Cross-sectional views focus on the TANF caseload at a given point in time. They may tell us what program activities or behavioral requirements active TANF clients are engaged in, or what their program status is (work-mandatory or work-exempt, for example). Cross-sectional descriptions may also describe what the current TANF caseload has accomplished while on TANF. Whatever the content, the focus of cross-sectional analysis in welfare reform research is usually the TANF caseload at a point in time.

Longitudinal analyses of program experiences are also useful in describing program operations and accomplishments. These types of analyses are concerned with change over time, and may adopt several different approaches. For example, they may be made up of successive cross-sectional views of the TANF caseload, allowing insights into whether and how the caseload is changing in composition (such as ethnicity, age, number of children) and/or behavior (such as employment). Another longitudinal perspective is afforded by following a group of clients over time and tracing their program paths and outcomes.

Both cross-sectional and longitudinal descriptions are useful in describing and assessing program implementation. The cross-sectional view affords descriptions of the status and program experiences of the active TANF caseload at a given point in time and addresses the question of what the TANF program and its clients look like and are doing at that time. The longitudinal view affords descriptions of how the TANF caseload has changed over time, or of the experiences and outcomes of a particular group of clients over time. Both views are critical to an understanding of "what is happening" in program implementation.

A logical place to begin describing program experiences and participation patterns is to ask what TANF clients are doing at a particular point in time, such as a reference month for the overall description of the program.[6] The question of whether and to what degree clients comply with program rules is particularly important in the current context of welfare reform in which most, if not all, adult TANF clients have some work-related or other behavioral requirement. It is a useful measure of a program's success to ask what proportion of clients are engaged in a specific allowable or required activity, such as job search, training, or unsubsidized employment.[7] Moreover, a large unexplained gap between the number of clients required to participate in a work activity and the actual number participating or being sanctioned for noncompliance may point to potential administrative issues that should be investigated by the implementation study.

Although the cross-sectional view is important for describing the level of training and work-related activity within the TANF caseload at a point in time, its perspective is relatively limited. For example, if some activities are required only once during a spell on TANF, or once over a given period, the point-in-time picture will not tell us how many clients have already satisfied this particular requirement. Moreover, because some administrative time is often needed to inform clients about required activities, and/or to assess and assign them to specific services, a snapshot of clients' statuses in a given week or month may not fairly assess the degree to which the program has encouraged compliance.

A more comprehensive approach to describing program experiences and participation patterns is to combine multiple perspectives to create an overall picture of what the program has accomplished over a given period, rather than how it looks at a point in time. A recent study of a JOBS program in Oregon uses this strategy effectively (Scrivener et al. 1998). First, the report presents data on the percentage of clients who attended a program orientation and participated in a work-related activity over the two years after the orientation (table 3.5). A subsequent table presents data on the length of time that clients participated in a JOBS activity during the two-year follow-up period (table 3.6). Finally, figure 3.4 combines the two perspectives in a way that summarizes the program's effectiveness in engaging JOBS-mandatory clients in a program activity or sanctioning them for noncompliance. The pie chart compares the amount of time JOBS-mandatory clients spent in four mutually exclusive and exhaustive statuses over the two-year follow-up period and thus allows some insight into how tightly the program was administered.[8]

Table 3.5, table 3.6, and figure 3.4 are examples of descriptions of the status or experiences of TANF participants at a point in time or summarized over a given period of time. Another way to describe client experiences is to show how experiences and statuses change over time. Figure 3.5 is an example from the same study of the Portland JOBS program that

Table 3.5. *Incidence of TANF Client Participation in Work-Related Activities over a Given Time Period*

National Evaluation of Welfare-to-Work Strategies:
Summary of Rates of Participation within a Two-Year Follow-Up Period,
Portland JOBS Program

Activity measure	Full participation sample (%)
Participated in:	
Any activity[a]	61.1
Job search[b]	42.7
Any education or training	30.3
Basic education	16.8
College	2.2
Vocational training	15.7
Life skills training	21.1
Work experience	4.3

Source: Adapted from Scrivener et al. (1998, 50).

[a]Includes participation in initial work search (IWS). Excluding IWS, the participation rate for the full sample is 59.5 percent.

[b]Includes participation in IWS. Excluding IWS, the participation rate for the full sample is 40.5 percent.

Table 3.6. *Length of TANF Client Participation in Work-Related Activities over a Given Time Period*

National Evaluation of Welfare-to-Work Strategies:
Length of Participation within a Two-Year Follow-Up Period, Portland JOBS Program

Activity measure	Full participation sample (months)
For all sample members for whom case files were reviewed:	
Average number of months receiving AFDC	14.5
Average number of months in which individuals were JOBS-mandatory[a]	12.4
Average number of months in which individuals participated in a JOBS activity	3.2

Source: Adapted from Scrivener et al. (1998, 52).

[a]A negligible portion of these months is accounted for by time during which clients were required to participate in initial work search before their AFDC grants were approved.

Figure 3.4. *Percentage of Time Clients Are Complying with Participation Requirements or Being Sanctioned*

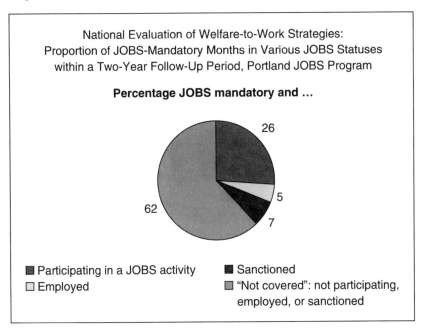

Source: Scrivener et al. (1998, 60).

shows how the proportion of clients in each of six mutually exclusive and exhaustive categories changed over the two-year follow-up period of the study. This perspective illustrates the point made in figure 3.4 in another way and adds information as well. That is, it shows first that over the follow-up period, most of the clients affected by the program have left the welfare rolls. Second, it illustrates that a relatively small proportion of JOBS-mandatory welfare clients at any time are either working or engaged in a JOBS activity.

Although figure 3.5 allows some insight into how a cohort of clients' program status changes over time, it does not give a detailed picture of how clients "flow" through a program. Programs that represent a series of decisions and/or activities that determine clients' passage are often described quantitatively by measuring how many clients take specific paths or reach a certain stage or end result. One example of how this can

Figure 3.5. *Change in Clients' Program Status over Time*

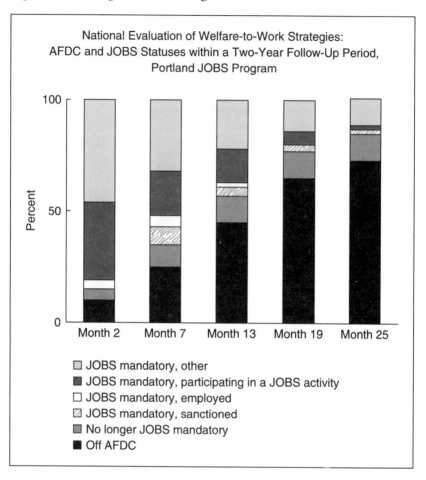

National Evaluation of Welfare-to-Work Strategies:
AFDC and JOBS Statuses within a Two-Year Follow-Up Period,
Portland JOBS Program

□ JOBS mandatory, other
■ JOBS mandatory, participating in a JOBS activity
□ JOBS mandatory, employed
▨ JOBS mandatory, sanctioned
■ No longer JOBS mandatory
■ Off AFDC

Source: Scrivener et al. (1998, 56).

be done is shown in figure 3.6, which tracks the program experiences of a group of clients since becoming subject to time-limited assistance in a welfare reform experiment in Florida. In the context of that study, it shows that relatively few clients ever actually reached their time limits within a certain period.

When a program is designed with a sequenced set of activities or services, program operators have an interest in knowing how many and

Figure 3.6. *Description of the Welfare Program Experiences and Outcomes of a Cohort of Clients*

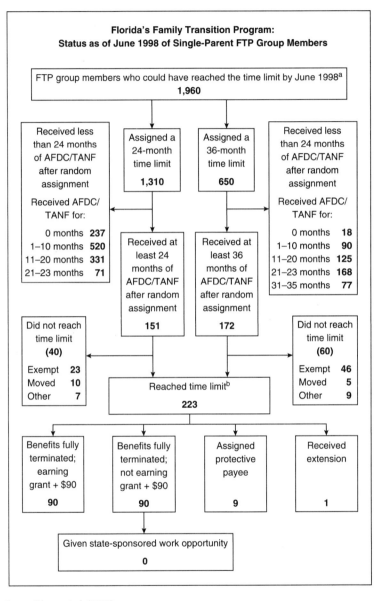

Florida's Family Transition Program:
Status as of June 1998 of Single-Parent FTP Group Members

FTP group members who could have reached the time limit by June 1998[a]
1,960

Received less than 24 months of AFDC/TANF after random assignment

Received AFDC/TANF for:

0 months	237
1–10 months	520
11–20 months	331
21–23 months	71

Assigned a 24-month time limit
1,310

Received at least 24 months of AFDC/TANF after random assignment
151

Assigned a 36-month time limit
650

Received at least 36 months of AFDC/TANF after random assignment
172

Received less than 24 months of AFDC/TANF after random assignment

Received AFDC/TANF for:

0 months	18
1–10 months	90
11–20 months	125
21–23 months	168
31–35 months	77

Did not reach time limit
(40)

Exempt	23
Moved	10
Other	7

Reached time limit[b]
223

Did not reach time limit
(60)

Exempt	46
Moved	5
Other	9

Benefits fully terminated; earning grant + $90
90

Benefits fully terminated; not earning grant + $90
90

Assigned protective payee
9

Received extension
1

Given state-sponsored work opportunity
0

Source: Bloom et al. (1999).

[a]This total includes all FTP group members with a 24-month time limit who enrolled between May 1994 and July 1996 and all FTP group members with a 36-month time limit who enrolled between May 1994 and July 1995.

[b]Of this group, three individuals were granted a four-month extension before their benefits were terminated.

what proportion of clients complete each step and achieve the desired goal of the program. A convenient approach to summarizing clients' progress in the program is illustrated in table 3.7, an excerpt from an implementation study of a welfare-to-work program that operated in Connecticut in the late 1980s. The table presents the probability that any client applying to be in the program will reach a given stage in the program (the column headings), as well as the conditional probability that once reaching a given stage, an applicant will move on to the next stages or outcomes in the process.

In the example in table 3.7, the probability that any applicant will complete the program and become employed as a "rollover" at the project site is 18 percent. For those applicants that made it to the first step in the program (pre-employment training [PET]), the probability is 25 percent, and for those placed at a job site, it is 60 percent. The table also illustrates the typical pattern of such programs—a relatively small percentage of individuals who begin ever actually complete all the steps leading to the desired outcome.

Client Outcomes

Another aspect of a human services program often described quantitatively is client outcomes. In pre-TANF research on welfare reform, the most com-

Table 3.7. *Progress of a Cohort of Clients through the Stages of an Employment and Training Program*

	Applicants (n = 445)	Enrolled in PET (%) (n = 332)	Placed in job (%) (n = 137)	Completed job placement (%) (n = 127)	Rolled over (%) (n = 82)
Subsidized Employment Programs Participant Flow (March 1987–June 1990): New Haven Site					
Applicants	–	75	31	29	18
PET enrollees	–	–	41	38	25
Job placements	–	–	–	93	60
Job completions	–	–	–	–	65

Source: Frees and Finkel (1991, 23).
Note: PET = pre-employment training.

mon outcomes measured were those most directly associated with the goals of reform: reducing dependency on cash assistance and increasing financial independence, usually through employment. Pre-TANF welfare reform programs, such as WIN or JOBS, also had other intermediate goals, such as increasing educational attainment or work experience.

More recent research on welfare reform has broadened the range of outcomes typically included in implementation studies of welfare programs. For example, general concern about the dramatic decrease in the welfare caseloads has led to a focus on how families are faring after leaving welfare. These so-called "leavers" studies have broadened the outcomes used to measure families' well-being beyond those outcomes typically associated with welfare reform research. Tables 3.8a and 3.8b are examples of specialized outcomes observed in studies of the TANF program. The first table shows outcomes associated with living arrangements included in a study of TANF leavers in the District of Columbia (Acs and Loprest 2001b). The second table is an example of a set of child outcomes observed for a study of TANF leavers in Massachusetts.

CHANGES IN OUTCOMES
While an implementation study can *describe* changes in client outcomes, only an impact study can *confirm* those changes as a function of the program or policies being studied. For example, observing changes in client

Table 3.8a. *Specialized Outcomes Observed in a TANF Leavers Study*

Living Arrangements of TANF Leavers in the District of Columbia: Survey Findings for Leavers from October to December, 1998	
Living arrangement	*Percentage*
Lives with spouse/partner	12.6
Got married/partnered	5.8
Got separated/divorced	6.9
Took in family/friends	16.6
Took in boarders	4.7
Moved in with family/friends	22.0
Children moved out	7.6
Children returned	4.7

Source: Acs and Loprest (2001b).

Table 3.8b. *Specialized Outcomes Observed in a TANF Leavers Study*

	Children's School Activity after Leaving Welfare (Children Age 6 to 17)		
Activity	Children in time limit closings (%) (n = 743)	Children in non–time limit closings (%) (n = 237)	Universe (%)
Attended classes for gifted students or did advanced work***	5.1	11.9	8.7
On sports team	36.9	38.0	37.5
Participated in extracurricular school activities	27.6	28.7	28.2
Participated in clubs/activities outside of school**	38.1	46.0	42.2
Suspended or expelled	11.5	13.5	12.5
Failed class or not promoted	13.3	15.6	14.5

Source: Massachusetts Department of Transitional Assistance (2000).

Note: The statistical significance levels of differences between the time limit closings and the non–time limit closings are indicated as ** = 5 percent, *** = 1 percent.

circumstances during or after a spell receiving welfare is a legitimate concern of implementation research on welfare reform. The danger lies in the temptation to ascribe all or some of those changes to policies and processes. Without a design to link changes in circumstances to new policies, it is normally not possible to distinguish between changes that are due to the program and those that are due to other causes and would have occurred in any case.[9]

Reporting Stakeholder Perspectives

Strictly speaking, the goal of the program narrative and relevant descriptive statistics is to present an objective account of "what is happening." In constructing the narrative, the researcher is in the role of a dispassionate, external observer. Also important for understanding why a program operates as it does and leads to the observed outcomes are the perspectives of program stakeholders. The stakeholders are those individuals—most notably program management, staff, and program participants—whose decisions and behaviors combine to form program experiences and outcomes. This section includes examples of descriptions of stakeholder perspectives based on data from surveys, focus groups, and ethnographic research and analysis, all of which enable us to enter the world of the program being studied.[10]

Survey Data

In addition to collecting information about program outcomes and experiences, survey questionnaires are often used to gather data about informants' attitudes, opinions, and program knowledge. For example, basic research using survey data to examine welfare clients' attitudes about work and welfare is often cited to support policies that enforce the obligation to work. In program evaluations of welfare reform, survey data on client awareness of new policies and philosophy can be useful in assessing the degree to which a program's rules and message have been communicated and absorbed by program participants. When compared with similar survey data from the past, results from more recent client surveys may help determine whether the culture of welfare and client expectations about entitlements have changed in the desired way.

Survey data can also be very helpful in measuring client satisfaction with program administration and services. Particularly as welfare agencies increasingly share program responsibilities with other agencies (such as workforce development agencies) or contract out for services with private firms, customer satisfaction surveys can help agencies assess the quality of services. Tables 3.9a and 3.9b show two examples of results from client surveys. The first is an example of responses to survey items testing clients' knowledge of program rules and services. The second is an example of survey results of clients' satisfaction with program services.

Worker surveys are used in program evaluations for similar reasons as client surveys. That is, they gauge the degree to which local office workers have absorbed new policies and program goals. For example, in most instances of welfare reform, agencies have undertaken ambitious attempts to alter basic program orientation and practices using the same workforce that operated older programs. Worker understanding of the new practices, acceptance of the new principles, and beliefs about the effectiveness of a welfare reform program can be key factors in its successful implementation. Table 3.10 is an example of a worker survey from an evaluation of Michigan's To Strengthen Michigan Families welfare reform program.

Table 3.9a. *Survey Results Measuring Client Understanding of Program Policies*

	Time-Limited Welfare: Percentage of Recipients Aware of Specific Program Rules in Florida and Vermont	
	Recipients aware of rule (%)	
Program rule	*Escambia County, Florida (n = 55)*	*Vermont (n = 47)*
I can keep more of AFDC check if I go to work.	53	70
I can own a car with no limit on how much it is worth.	35	75
I can have more savings and still receive AFDC.	53	66
There is a time limit to how long I can receive AFDC.	84	98
Child support payments are sent to me instead of the welfare department.	n.a.	51
I am required to talk with the teacher from my children's school during each grading period.	71	n.a.
I am required to provide proof that my preschool children have been immunized.	78	n.a.
I am required to participate in Project Independence (Florida's JOBS program) to get education, training, or help in finding a job.	86	n.a.

Source: Bloom and Butler (1995, 5).

Notes: Surveys were administered two to three months after participants entered the programs. Respondents could give more than one response; therefore, distributions could add to more than 100 percent.

n.a. = not applicable.

Focus Groups

Short-answer survey questionnaires that measure stakeholder attitudes and opinions allow researchers to make statistical analyses and draw generalizations about the universe represented by the survey sample. However, it is difficult to scratch beneath the surface of the close-ended responses for more depth and for the rationales behind those opinions. In this regard, focus group discussions offer some advantages as well as disadvantages. While focus group discussions allow participants to more fully express and develop their views, focus group results are usually not

Table 3.9b. *Survey Results Measuring Client Assessment of Program Services*

Respondents' Perceptions of the Ways in Which JOBS Has Been Helpful					
	Clients giving free response (%)				
	Minneapolis (n = 100)	*Utica (n = 100)*	*Springfield (n = 57)*	*Houston (n = 99)*	*Total (N = 356)*
Assistance in getting and paying for education and training	38.3	57.0	66.8	54.1	52.5
Assistance in getting and paying for child care	37.3	17.0	1.8	19.0	23.6
Increasing confidence, self-esteem, and motivation	18.1	22.0	52.7	26.1	27.1
Clarifying and helping to reach goals	13.0	36.0	10.6	21.1	21.4
Assistance in getting and paying for transportation	26.0	2.0	1.8	11.0	11.2
Support	15.1	9.0	15.9	4.0	10.4

Source: Hagen and Lurie (1994a, 86).

amenable to statistical manipulation and are not necessarily representative of any larger group.

Well-organized focus groups are usually directed by a moderator using a topic guide to help shape the discussion. Just as the interview guides used to collect program information may serve as templates for organizing data into a descriptive narrative, the focus group moderator guides can also help organize accounts of the discussion. Focus groups are often summarized along the main points discussed within each topic heading with direct quotations from participants to add emphasis and flavor. Figure 3.7 is a section of a report describing the focus group discussions of clients in a welfare reform program in Arizona called EMPOWER.

Table 3.10. *Survey Results Measuring Staff Acceptance and Assessment of Program Policies and Services*

Selected Results of Worker Survey about the To Strengthen Michigan Families Welfare Reform Program	

Survey question	Worker responses (%)
Are there sufficient opportunities for clients to:	
Enroll in employment and training programs?	Yes: 66 No: 34
Enroll in education programs?	Yes: 86 No: 14
Volunteer in community service activities?	Yes: 83 No: 17
Volunteer in employment?	Yes: 57 No: 43
Work part time?	Yes: 80 No: 20
Work full time?	Yes: 56 No: 44
How would you rate the adequacy of resources available to Michigan DSS to implement TSMF program changes successfully?	Inadequate: 40 Somewhat inadequate: 25 Satisfactory: 33 Somewhat adequate: 4 Adequate: 2
How has worker morale been affected by the implementation of TSMF?	Declined: 21 Declined somewhat: 21 Same: 48 Improved somewhat: 6 Improved: 4

Source: Hargreaves, Werner, and Joshi (1995, appendix C).

Figure 3.7. *Focus Group Summary*

Participant Perceptions of Life after Cash Assistance

Participants were nearly unanimous in asserting that they are, in general, better off since leaving cash assistance. Most have increased their household incomes, although modestly in many cases, and they feel more secure in general. Employment has provided other benefits: participants have experienced an increase in self-esteem, and they are proud that they can support their families without relying either at all or as heavily on public benefits. For others, receipt of child support and disability benefits have provided more substantial support. Other benefits of being off cash assistance and being able to "make it on your own" are "renewed determination," being a better role model for children, and reduced stigma. As one participant explained, *"I felt ashamed when I was on welfare."*

Participants offered strong comments about the trade-offs of being more self-sufficient. Most notably, some of these parents lamented the dramatic decrease in the amount of time they could spend with their children. Women holding more than one job and those balancing work with school felt this most severely. These comments illustrate their concerns:

"We are better off, but in another way, I'm not doing as well. I work so much and go to school. We have our own house, but then again, I hardly ever see my kids. Although we have a little bit of extra money, we don't have time."

"My family doesn't want for anything now. However, quality time with my kids is limited. When I'm with them, we need to spend time on homework, baths...That's about it."

"It's so hard when you are on your own, trying to be both a mother and a father. Harder when you're working. There's no one to help you."

When asked about "the best part" of being off cash assistance, participants offered these comments:

"It's a good feeling to know that you're making it on your own."
"You have more pride."
"You have your self esteem and your dignity."
"If you feel better about yourself, and you're a better parent."
"Your children respect you. You can be a better role model."
"You don't have to sit at a DES office for hours."

Source: Diane Porcari, focus group field report from Evaluation of Arizona's EMPOWER Welfare reform program. Cambridge, Abt Associates Inc., 1998.

What place do focus group results have in descriptive analysis in implementation research? Perhaps the best way to answer this question is to begin with what focus groups do not provide. Most importantly, they do not provide data that may be confidently generalized to a larger group. The discussants are most often volunteers who are sampled for "convenience" and not to make inferences to a larger population. Moreover, the discussion may not even be representative of the members of the group itself. Some focus groups may be dominated by one or two strong personalities; more reserved members may shrink from contradicting the louder voices. Although a skillful moderator should be able to bring out contending views when they exist, the "chemistry" may not exist for a free and open discussion.

The foregoing reservations notwithstanding, focus groups may be useful for descriptive analysis in two major ways.[11] First, they can provide a "reality check" on results based on other data collection methods. That is, focus groups can test grounds for conclusions based on surveys or open-ended interviews about how group members feel and think. Second, focus group results may help add a deeper texture to our understanding of how key stakeholders feel about program policies, services, and philosophies. By allowing those stakeholders to put in their own words how they are affected by program changes, successful focus groups can add a powerful personal dimension to program descriptions.

In-Depth Interviews and Ethnographic Research

Focus group discussions allow some insight into how stakeholders view program changes in policies, services, and philosophy within the larger context of their lives.[12] In-depth interviews and ethnographic research afford even greater detail by "entering" the world of those stakeholders while collecting data. In its most intensive form, ethnographic research often entails extensive contact with the social group being studied and may include a period of residence in the same location. In this way, researchers attempt to experience directly the social reality of the group being studied.

Ethnographic studies have a useful, if limited place, in implementation research. They may be particularly relevant in studies that seek to monitor the goals of institutional and cultural change associated with new program or policy initiatives. To address these issues fully, researchers may need to use the techniques of ethnography to "get inside" the world of the program participant or staff to understand whether and how the new approach has been integrated into their "worldview." The stakeholders' subjective viewpoint is precisely the goal of this type of ethnographic research. The case for this type of approach in policy research and evaluation is stated eloquently in a study of the income-generating strategies of poor single mothers (Edin and Lein 1997, 18–19):

> We believe that the in-depth accounts of these 379 single mothers' real-life economic situations and the survival strategies they employed to resolve these situations can shed new light on welfare reform efforts across states. In the scholarly debate about welfare reform, the voices and lived experiences of single mothers are often drowned out by reams of statistics, usually aggregate numbers that, while useful, can distance us from the daily struggles poor single women face as they try to both parent and provide for their children.

Findings from ethnographic studies are usually organized and presented in implementation study reports in two related ways. Relevant stories about individual clients or workers may be woven into vignettes to illustrate points made in statistical analyses or to typify clients' situations or behaviors. In this way, the results are secondary to other analytic tools and are used simply to put "flesh" on the numbers.

In the other approach, ethnographic findings are used as primary data to develop hypotheses about how and why clients may react to policy initiatives. Rather than providing stories to illustrate results derived from statistical data, this more direct approach helps create an explanatory context in which to understand the quantitative data. This use of ethnographic findings (based on intensive, multiple interviews) is well illustrated in figure 3.8, which includes a passage from a chapter entitled "Why Don't Welfare-Reliant Mothers Go to Work?" in Edin and Lein (1997, 65–67).

Linking Descriptive Analysis Strategies with Research Questions

This chapter reviewed descriptive strategies available to implementation research. Table 3.11 links our set of basic implementation study research questions with those strategies. Note that the questions that require evaluative or explanatory analysis are not included in table 3.11, which deals exclusively with program description.

Figure 3.8. *Using Ethnographic Data to Develop Hypotheses*

"A Total Trap"

One Boston woman had only recently gone on welfare after seven years of working as a police dispatcher. Her top wage at this job was $7 an hour—a relatively high wage compared with the other women in our sample. She made ends meet on this wage only because she had a housing subsidy and a live-in boyfriend who paid a lot of the expenses. Despite the fact that she worked full time, she could not afford to move out of the projects. After her boyfriend left and stopped contributing to her budget, she could not pay her bills. Thus, after seven years, she returned to welfare and went back to school:

> There's nothing in a low salary job because ... your rent be so high ... you know, people don't believe that people who work and live in the projects be paying $400–$500 for rent. But that's true because you can't really afford—for three bedroom, you can't really afford to go out and be paying $1,000 for a private apartment. You go out and get a job and then they take your rent subsidy away from you. You pay that much rent and it's hard just trying to maintain the low standard of living you had on welfare. You're in the same position, so it don't matter if you're working or not.

.... Another mother spoke of the combined effect of losing medical coverage, food stamps, and part of her housing subsidy when she took her last job as a housekeeper for a cleaning service:

> They say that they want mothers to get off the aid and work, okay. There's a lot of mothers who want to work, okay, like me. I want to work. And then you work, they don't give you a medical card. And sometimes, it depends on how much you make, they cut off your medical card, and when you go out and get those jobs you don't make enough money to pay rent, then medical coverage and bills. It not really worth it to go out working when you think about it, you know ... You're losing double.

.... Apart from believing that working was a financial wash, women also felt they would gain little self-respect from the minimum-wage jobs they could get with their current skills. Nearly all of our welfare-reliant respondents said they would feel better about themselves if they could make it without welfare, but this boost to their self-esteem seemed to depend on a working life that offered somewhat higher wages and better prospects for advancement than they thought they could get with their current skills and job experience.

Source: Edin and Lein (1997, 65–67).

Table 3.11. *Illustrative Implementation Study Research Questions and Descriptive Analysis Strategies*

Research domain and questions	Descriptive analysis strategies
Theoretical and practical basis	
How was the program planned and developed?	• Narrative description based on documents, open-ended interviews
What general and specific goals is the program designed to meet? Are they feasible?	• Narrative description based on documents, open-ended interviews
How are the program's prescribed policies, procedures, activities, and services designed to advance the program's general and specific goals?	• Program conceptual ("logic") model
External program environment	
What are the demographic, social, cultural, political, and economic environments in which the program operates?	• Narrative description based on documents, open-ended interviews, surveys, focus groups, on-site observations • Descriptive statistics
In what ways has the program's environment affected its implementation, operations, and results?	• Narrative description based on documents, open-ended interviews
Are the necessary resources to operate the program in place?	
Are all required resources available?	• Narrative description based on documents, open-ended interviews
Which resources are in short supply and why? How does this vary by locality?	• Narrative description based on documents, open-ended interviews • Descriptive statistics
What implications does the level of resources have for program operations and performance?	• Narrative description based on documents, open-ended interviews • Descriptive statistics
Are program processes and systems operating as planned?	
Are all program processes and systems operating as planned? Does this vary by locality?	• Narrative description based on documents, open-ended interviews • Descriptive statistics

(continued)

Table 3.11. *Continued*

Research domain and questions	Descriptive analysis strategies
Is the program reaching the intended target population?	
How many clients are scheduled for various program activities and services? What proportion of clients scheduled for program activities and services attend as scheduled? What other services are clients using?	• Narrative description based on open-ended interviews, observations, surveys, focus groups • Descriptive statistics
What are the content and quality of program activities and services?	• Narrative description based on open-ended interviews, observations, surveys, focus groups
What are the implications of the content, timing, and quality of services for program operations and performance? How does this vary by locality? How may services be improved?	• Narrative description based on open-ended interviews, observations, surveys, focus groups
Is the program achieving desired outcomes?	
What are the relevant outcomes of program clients? What are the changes in their overall well-being?	• Descriptive statistics • Narrative description based on open-ended interviews, surveys, focus groups, ethnographic research

NOTES

1. In using the terms "program narrative" and "descriptive statistics," we avoid the sometimes confusing distinction between qualitative and quantitative research. Sometimes implementation research is referred to as "qualitative research." In fact, however, it is difficult to see how implementation research can be conducted successfully without collecting and organizing quantitative information.

2. Miles and Huberman (1984) describe a similar, if more formal, activity called an "analysis meeting." It is applied chiefly to the task of fleshing out what is happening in an individual site that has been visited by multiple researchers.

3. In part, the lack of communication between the two agencies was a holdover from pre-TANF days. In fact, shortly after this study was begun, the Arizona Department of Economic Security redesigned service delivery to colocate Department of Human Resources (DHR) and DES workers in the same offices.

4. For a fuller and slightly different treatment of this issue, see Wolcott (1994, 17–23).

5. The table is based on a more extensive table of the characteristics of a research sample of clients from the Manpower Demonstration Research Corporation evaluation of Florida's Family Transition Program. See Bloom et al. (1999, 16–17).

6. For example, the month in which the study made field visits to program sites.

7. For example, implementation evaluations of the JOBS Program showed that many program participants were engaged in an educational activity, such as Adult Basic Education or English as a Second Language. While such activities may be important prerequisites to employment, the relatively heavy involvement in these services led some critics of JOBS to conclude that the program was not moving enough clients quickly enough into employment.

8. Note that the patterns displayed in the pie chart are typical of welfare-to-work programs in which a sizable portion of work-mandatory clients are waiting to be assigned to, or to begin some activity, or are apparently noncompliant but have not yet been sanctioned.

9. The rare exception is when a program supplies services or resources not normally available *and* only those resources or services could possibly have led to a change in outcomes. An example would be a new vaccine for a disease previously not preventable. It is likely that decreases in the incidence of the disease after a mass inoculation could be largely attributable to the new vaccine. This situation is extremely rare in the context of a welfare reform program or policies.

10. Note that these data collection techniques are described in chapter 2. Here, the emphasis is on how the results may be organized in describing stakeholder views.

11. Note that focus groups may also be useful in designing the research approach and data collection instruments; see chapter 2.

12. In this section we discuss in-depth interviews and ethnography as ways to describe how welfare reform programs interact with clients lives; "street-level bureaucracy" is discussed in chapter 4.

4

Assessing and Explaining Implementation

The previous chapter presented implementation research strategies for organizing and analyzing data to address the question "What is happening?" (documenting implementation). This chapter discusses the range of approaches used to tie together comprehensive descriptions to help assess and explain program implementation, addressing the questions: "Is it what is expected or desired?" (assessing implementation) and "Why is it happening as it is?" (explaining implementation).

As discussed in chapter 1, assessing implementation and explaining implementation mean different things. Assessing a program's implementation implies rating it against some set of expectations, program models, or standards. Explaining a program's implementation implies developing plausible causal explanations for program operations and results, or addressing the question of why the program operates and performs as it does. Moreover, explanation often proceeds within the framework of some theory about how the program should work or about how the program's larger environment and structure may affect its operations and results.

Assessing Implementation

Assessing program implementation is clearly one of the central missions of evaluation research and is the means by which legislators, policymakers, program administrators, and the general public learn about the success of a given intervention. As discussed in chapter 1, researchers generally distinguish between implementation (or process) and impact evaluations. The goal of an impact evaluation is to discover whether a given policy or social intervention is making a difference, as well as how much of a difference and for whom. Impact evaluations accomplish their mission by comparing *what happens* within the context of the policy or intervention being tested with *what would have happened* in the absence of the policy or intervention, or the "counterfactual."

Assessments of implementation also compare data on program operations, activities, services, and outcomes with some set of models, norms, or standards. However, unlike an impact evaluation, an implementation study may require multiple comparisons. The challenge for program assessments is to select the appropriate models, standards, or norms that define "what is expected or desired." In chapter 1, we listed the most common types of standards:

- *Program model, plan, or design.* This is the blueprint for the program and may include specifications of a program's policies, services, target population, and expected short- and long-term outcomes.
- *Federal and state legislative or administrative rules specifying program content and performance standards.* These are general guidelines and expectations about program content, participation, and outcomes that may apply to multiple program models and approaches. For example, the national welfare reform legislation creating TANF mandated the development of federal standards for the proportion of welfare clients participating in work-related activities that may trigger penalties or incentive payments to states. The standards apply to all state TANF programs, regardless of specific policy and service choices.
- *Broader social standards.* In some instances, success in program implementation or outcomes may be judged by broader social standards. For example, one way to assess the success of welfare reform programs is to measure the number of welfare families that leave welfare and achieve incomes above the poverty line.
- *Industry standards or exemplary programs.* Other related types of benchmarks or norms sometimes used in implementation research are industry standards or exemplary programs. Industry standards are formal or informal norms for program content or performance

based on a general consensus of what constitutes an effective program and what level of performance is expected. For example, the American Public Welfare Association (now, the American Public Human Services Association) several years ago developed guidelines (not rigorous professional standards) for case management for the JOBS Program (see American Public Human Services Association 1993, 1994). Exemplary programs are related to this type of standard. For example, in the wake of its overwhelmingly positive results in an impact evaluation, the Riverside County "Work First" approach to welfare reform was often invoked as a national model for program content and performance.

- *Professional experience and judgment.* Implementation researchers may also use their own judgment to assess various aspects of program operations and results. Researcher judgment may be based on a variety of factors, including research experience and knowledge of similar programs.
- *Stakeholder opinions and judgments.* Program operators, participants, and other stakeholders can contribute valuable perspectives on the quality of program policies, operations, and services.

A program assessment may differ greatly according to the standards chosen for the evaluation study. For example, while many post-TANF welfare programs have met or exceeded federal standards for work participation among TANF clients, they have not done as well in lifting families out of poverty. Similarly, although many welfare programs have been implemented as planned by state policymakers and program operators, they may not have been as successful in satisfying the expectations or needs of TANF program stakeholders.

Because a program assessment relies on the standard against which implementation is judged, the choice of standards is important, and should be defensible by researchers. It may be argued that the "fairest" standards are those set by program plans and expectations, and that programs should only be judged in their own terms. This is usually the chief concern of state and federal government agencies, the most frequent funders of large-scale evaluation research. Nevertheless, implementation researchers may sometimes wish to consider other perspectives when evaluating programs or policies in a broader context. Moreover, researchers may need to compare implementation results across programs and by reference to a set of similar standards that transcend specific program design.

In any event, the standards used to assess program implementation are not immutable, and may themselves come into question. They may not be appropriate to specific program applications, they may be overly optimistic or pessimistic in their expectations for program results, or they may be based on flawed theories or poor empirical research. Ultimately, the usefulness of any evaluative standard turns on its acceptance by the researcher, policymaker, and program practitioner communities; the objectivity and reliability of its application across multiple programs; and its ability to guide practical decisions about future program design and administration.

The remainder of this section discusses each of the evaluative standards listed above and illustrates their uses in implementation research.

Program Model, Plan, or Design

Among the most common standards used in assessing program implementation are programs' design and expectations. This is particularly true when the program model is a design that has already been shown to be feasible and effective. When policymakers and program operators have sound reasons for implementing a given set of policies and services, they first want to know if the implementation is faithful to the blueprints. Moreover, judging the success of a program (or policy, or service, or administrative approach) in its own terms has a certain face validity as an objective way to assessing program implementation. Finally, for some evaluation approaches (most notably "theory of change," discussed below), the program's design and expected short- and long-term outcomes are the sole standards against which to assess implementation success fairly.

A recent evaluation study of efforts to improve the quantity and quality of child care for low-income families provides a good example of the use of detailed program plans as the major evaluative criteria for judging the success of program implementation. The first step in the research project entailed developing detailed program models and expectations with the help of program managers and staff at the various project sites. Like the example presented in figure 3.2, the models expose the ways in which program structure, activities, and services are hypothesized to lead to program goals. The evaluation consisted largely in the periodic observation of project activities and results and a comparison of actual program experience with the detailed program models. Figure 4.1 illustrates this approach as used to evaluate the success of

Figure 4.1. *Evaluating Program Implementation Using a Program Model as a Standard*

SITE X GOAL 1

Desired systemic change	Strategies/activities
Create a self-sustaining network of high-quality family child care homes	Conduct a violence-prevention conference (attended by some child care providers)
	Meet with providers attending the conference to promote quality care and discuss the formation of a provider association
	Conduct a broad-based child care conference to promote quality and recruit homes for the providers' association
	Establish an organizational structure and develop a business plan

Research findings in report text

Overall, Site X's initiative does not appear to be implementing its strategies for forming a providers association as planned. No progress has been made on the development of an organizational structure or business plan for the association. Thus far, there has been little, if any, meaningful outreach to providers in county X. It is difficult to recruit providers to join an association that has no clear mission or agenda.

....The strategy has now been changed—rather than forming a single countywide association, separate associations will be formed in each of four parts of the county.

(*continued*)

Figure 4.1. *Continued*

SITE X GOAL 2

Desired systemic change	Strategies/activities
Create a system for improving the quality of child care	Community outreach to identify potential new child care providers
	Develop community quality standards with appropriate training materials and assessment tools
	Conduct monthly training sessions for potential providers
	Assist new providers with the licensure process
	Assess the quality of new providers and providers that are association members with targeted training/technical assistance as needed
	Publicize quality standards in the community

Research findings in report text

The goal to increase the supply of quality care in the county has not been fully achieved.... The first step toward achieving this goal was to identify a pool of 100 potential new providers in the county. This was to be accomplished by conducting monthly open houses.... This activity did not take place as planned.

The initiative has had somewhat more success in developing local quality standards for child care. A consultant was hired to develop a set of community quality standards and assessment tools. The standards were developed, but the assessment tools that were developed cannot be used to assess quality objectively.

.... There do not appear to be any realistic plans to try to attain the desired goal of creating a system in county X to improve the quality of child care.

Source: Unpublished project notes from an Abt Associates' study of child care for low-income families.

a project site in implementing strategies and activities prescribed by its program model.

Program models or designs may also prescribe quantitative goals, such as goals for participation or client outcomes. In these instances, program assessments may appear to be straightforward comparisons of program results with program goals. However, researchers should take care to specify definitions of observed activities or outcomes, such as "participation in a work-related activity" and "entered employment," for example. The specifications for these measures may differ by intensity (such as "hours per week") or length of time (such as number of weeks or months). The measures used by researchers should be defined the same way as those detailed in program plans or goals.

Table 4.1 is an example of an assessment of program implementation using quantitative measures. The exhibit is from an evaluation of an early welfare-to-work program in New York State using intensive services and case management, the Comprehensive Employment Opportunities Service Center (CEOSC) program. Each site projected participation levels for various services or activities. The exhibit indicates how many of the project sites met their "numbers" for participation in specific program services or activities.

Table 4.1. *Evaluating Program Implementation Using Quantitative Program Goals as Standards*

Success in Meeting Participation Goals in the CEOSC Program			
Program activity or service	*Number of sites subject to benchmark*	*Number of sites meeting benchmark*	*Number of sites meeting 75 percent of benchmark*
Opportunity contract	9	5	7
Preemployment training	7	6	7
Educational training	3	2	3
Skills training	5	3	3
Combined educational and skills training	4	4	4
Total	28	20	24

Source: Werner and Nutt-Powell (1988).

Federal and State Legislative or Administrative Rules Specifying Program Content and Performance Standards

Often, legislation creating social programs specifies or mandates lead agencies to develop standards for program content, participation, and outcomes. Moreover, meeting or exceeding participation or outcome standards often results in bonus funding, while failing to meet the standards may result in penalties; this is the case for state-level work participation rates for TANF recipients, for example. The standards usually impose the same set of expectations on multiple program implementations and so allow for meaningful comparisons across programs.

The legislation creating the Even Start Family Literacy Program in 1989 required that all local projects provide a set of basic program elements, including core instructional elements and support services. The requirements stop short of specifying curriculum and leave the details to individual project sites. An obvious issue for the evaluation of Even Start was to measure the degree to which projects met the minimum standards for program content. Table 4.2 summarizes the degree to which Even Start projects met the specific program content requirements.

Legislatively or administratively mandated participation levels are a relatively common way to impose overarching performance standards. Table 4.3 presents an example of the use of participation standards in an implementation evaluation of the Job Opportunity and Basic Skills (JOBS) program.

Performance standards are sometimes applied to program outcomes. For example, the national welfare reform legislation passed in 1996—the Personal Responsibility and Work Opportunities Reconciliation Act (PRWORA)—established bonus payments to states that lowered their rates of out-of-wedlock births by a given percentage. Sometimes, specific benchmarks are adjusted for local conditions that may affect outcomes regardless of the program's performance. For example, performance standards for employment outcomes for the now obsolete Job Training Partnership Act (JTPA) program were adjusted for local economic conditions.

Broader Social Standards

Public interest in a program or a set of social policies may extend beyond the performance standards for participation and outcomes set

Table 4.2. *Evaluating Program Implementation Using Legislatively Mandated Standards for Program Content*

Percentage of Projects That Met, Did Not Meet, and Had Missing Data for Even Start's Legislatively Mandated Program Elements (Based on 700 Projects in 1998–1999)

Program element	Met the requirement (%)	Did not meet the requirement (%)	Missing data (%)
Identify and recruit families most in need of services	98	<1	2
Screen and prepare families who then participate fully in Even Start	94	2	4
Accommodate family schedules and provide support services	96	1	3
Provide high quality instructional programs of sufficient intensity	See separate analysis		
Provide staff with ongoing training	Not available in 1998–1999 program data		
Provide some home-based instructional services	93	2	5
Provide year-round services	91	3	6
Build on community resources to avoid duplication of services	97	0	3
Serve families most in need and provide tailored services	Same as #1		
Participate in independent local evaluation	97	1	2
Serve children in at least a three-year age range	Not available in 1998–1999 program data		
All program elements	83	7	10

Source: St. Pierre et al. (2000, 4–46).

Table 4.3. *Use of Federal Participation Standards as an Evaluative Benchmark*

Mandatory AFDC Cases and JOBS Participation Rates, Selected Months 1992

Site	AFDC cases	Mandatory cases	Mandatory cases (%)	1992 participation rate (%)
Maryland	77,719	38,355	49	10.5
Baltimore	40,428	7,517	19	
Anne Arundel	3,474	382	11	
Dorchester	683	299	44	
Michigan	224,462	129,850	58	18.0
Wayne	93,814	n.a.		
Kalamazoo	4,548	n.a.		
Tuscola	1,098	n.a.		
Mississippi	20,304	9,595	47	14.1
Hinds	5,715	2,743	48	
Harrison	2,319	1,113	48	
Quitman	414	199	48	
New York	397,820	169,843	43	15.1
New York City	251,948	110,645	44	
Oneida	3,428	1,566	46	
Franklin	700	391	56	

Source: Hagen and Lurie (1994b, 221, 223).
Note: n.a. = not applicable

forth in legislation or in a program's administrative rules and guidelines. This is particularly true in the case of welfare reform. Indeed, the debate surrounding the passage of national welfare reform legislation went far beyond setting benchmarks for the TANF work participation rate. Among the broader goals associated with welfare reform are decreases in poverty and out-of-wedlock births, and increases in child support payments.

An example of research concerned with broader social measures and standards in evaluating welfare reform are the so-called "leavers studies." Those studies have focused on the post-TANF experience of families that have exited welfare since national welfare reform. Included among the many outcome measures observed are poverty rates and instances of hardship since leaving welfare. Table 4.4 is an example of outcome measures of material hardship before and after leaving TANF from a synthesis report on a selected group of leavers studies. (Note that leavers studies are a specialized type of implementation research that focuses on the outcomes experienced by program participants. They are not impact studies, as they make no attempt to link outcomes to policies, services, or administrative practices.)

Industry Standards or Exemplary Programs

Industry standards are quantitative and qualitative measures of individual worker, local office, or program activity output; codes of conduct; or any other performance-related benchmarks or expectations. In welfare reform programming, for example, such standards could potentially establish ranges of reasonable worker caseloads, a set of best practices for casework, or national certification standards for TANF caseworkers. While industry standards are widely used in other professions, such as medicine, education, accounting, children's services, and law, however,

Table 4.4. *Use of Broader Social Standards as an Evaluative Benchmark*

Leavers' Experience of Material Hardship: Survey Data		
	Washington State	
	Past 6 months on TANF (%)	*Past 6 months— leavers (%)*
Cut size of/skipped meals sometimes or often	39	43
Child skipped meal	5	4
Went without food all day at least once	11	15
Received food from food bank/shelter	35	44
Forced to move because could not meet housing costs	3	7
Without place to live at least once	11	13
Stayed in homeless shelter	2	1
Utilities cut off for failure to pay	12	12
Children in foster care	2	3

Source: Acs and Loprest (2001a, 25–26).

they have rarely been developed in the administration of cash assistance or welfare-to-work programs.

One possible reason for the lack of industry standards in TANF programs is that the job of an eligibility worker—the most common type of worker in TANF programs—is different across states and even across local or county offices within the same state. Both the policies guiding casework and the level of professional skill and responsibility required by the job may differ depending on the circumstances. However, as TANF programs focus increasingly on the expanding role of the caseworker in identifying clients' barriers to employment, linking them with appropriate services, and monitoring their progress toward economic independence, industry standards have a greater rationale and basis in practice.[1]

Far more common than industry standards are references to exemplary programs and program performance. For example, while an impact evaluation of the California Greater Avenues for Independence (GAIN) program found evidence of the program's effectiveness in all six study counties, it found particularly impressive results for Riverside County (Riccio, Friedlander, and Freedman 1994, 292–94). For example, the Riverside GAIN program produced both earnings gains and welfare savings, and was the only study county to have positive benefit-cost ratios from both participant and government perspectives.

The findings for Riverside GAIN became particularly important in two major ways in the welfare reform debates preceding the passage of PRWORA. First, they demonstrated that it was possible to design and implement a welfare-to-work program in which "everybody wins," thereby raising expectations (and implied benchmarks) for other welfare-to-work programs. Second, the results focused attention on those aspects of the Riverside GAIN program that seemed to explain its success. By comparing in a nonstatistical way contextual, administrative, and operational similarities and differences among the six GAIN study counties, the study's authors were able to develop hypotheses about why Riverside GAIN achieved its results (Riccio et al. 1994; also see Riccio and Hasenfeld 1996). One of the most important observations was that Riverside's philosophical and administrative emphasis on rapid placement in a job, regardless of a client's work skills, experience, or educational attainment, was a distinctive program feature that likely had something to do with its relative success. This hypothesis seemed to make sense, and seemed to be mirrored in worker and client perspectives on the Riverside program. The exemplary performance of Riverside GAIN has helped lead to a wide adoption of the "Work First" model of welfare reform in many other states and counties.

Professional Experience and Judgment

Sometimes a program may be unique or entirely new, without a specific program model, set of performance standards, or direct prior program experience against which it may be evaluated. In these instances, implementation researchers may need to call upon their knowledge of prior research and experience in assessing similar programs to develop a frame of reference for evaluation.

A common application of this approach is to develop lessons about exemplary program models, or "best practices," based on the assessment of experts in the field. For example, in a report titled *Model Strategies in Bilingual Education,* McCollum and Russo (1993) compile profiles of "nine exemplary sites, selected with the assistance of a panel of experts, which exhibit a wide range of parent involvement and family literacy programs." This type of research product can then inform the expansion of a new or innovative service. An important drawback of the expert opinion approach is that the standards used often represent one or a limited number of perspectives on what constitutes best practices. These types of research findings are strongest when backed up by more objective standards of program performance.

Stakeholder Opinions and Judgment

A final set of evaluative standards for assessing program implementation are stakeholder opinions and judgments. Those closest to program operations and results—most notably program participants and frontline workers—often have a privileged, if sometimes heavily biased, view of how well a program is working.

The previous chapter discussed gathering information about stakeholder attitudes and opinions as a *descriptive* exercise, or as a set of facts about the program environment and broader cultural context. But stakeholder opinions also have potential validity as assessment tools, if applied with caution and with some insight into what counts as "successful implementation" for each stakeholder group or perspective. From the point of view of policymakers and agency managers, such stakeholder assessments may be valuable tools for targeting resources needed to improve program operations and results.

A client survey from the National Evaluation of Welfare-to-Work Strategies included client assessments of specific implementation issues and program effectiveness (Scrivener et al. 1998, 135–36). Table 4.5 presents selected items from the survey.

A survey for the evaluation of the To Strengthen Michigan Families (TSMF) welfare reform program included some questions asking workers to assess the program's effectiveness and quality and level of implementation (Hargreaves et al. 1995). Table 4.6 summarizes some of the findings from the survey.

Table 4.5. *Use of Client Perspectives in Evaluating Program Implementation*

National Evaluation of Welfare-to-Work Strategies: Selected Client Survey Measures

Measure	Atlanta HCD	Atlanta LFA	Grand Rapids HCD	Grand Rapids LFA
Personalized attention and encouragement				
Percentage who feel their JOBS case manager knows a lot about them and their family	29.1	39.7	38.7	47.4
Percentage who believe JOBS staff would help them resolve problems that affected their participation in JOBS	42.5	44.1	27.7	25.9
Rule enforcement and sanctioning				
Percentage who say they were informed about penalties for noncompliance	68.8	67.9	82.4	80.9
Percentage who felt the JOBS staff just wanted to enforce the rules	52.0	57.4	63.8	71.8
Perceptions of effectiveness of JOBS				
Percentage who think the program improved their long-run chances of getting or keeping a job	39.3	39.4	28.0	30.5
Sample size	1,113	804	574	574

Source: Scrivener et al. (1998, 135–36).

Notes: HCD = Human Capital Development program model; LFA = Labor Force Attachment program model.

Table 4.6. *Use of Worker Perspectives in Evaluating Program Implementation*

Selected Responses from Worker Survey from the Evaluation of
To Strengthen Michigan Families

Survey item	Responses (%)
Please rate the quality and appropriateness of the training you received:	
Excellent	9
Good	51
Fair	28
Poor	11
How has worker morale been affected by the implementation of TSMF?	
Declined	21
Declined somewhat	21
Same	48
Improved somewhat	6
Improved	4
In your opinion, how likely will TSMF change	
Your office's service orientation?	
Not at all likely	8
Somewhat unlikely	5
No difference	42
Somewhat likely	35
Likely	11
Clients' attitudes toward welfare?	
Not at all likely	8
Somewhat unlikely	6
No difference	49
Somewhat likely	30
Likely	7

Source: Hargreaves et al. (1995).

Explaining Implementation

From a practical point of view, explaining program implementation—understanding why a program is operating and performing as it is—can be a particularly useful part of implementation research. In explaining implementation, researchers try to expose the reasons that programs are not working as expected so that policymakers and program operators can make needed adjustments. Moreover, it is through explanation that researchers try to uncover why successful programs work well, so that their lessons may be used to fix other program sites or to guide future program replication.

Although explaining program implementation can be useful, it can also be controversial and difficult. The general reason is that explanation implies causation. To explain something in social science is to make a claim about causality. Hypothesizing about causal connections in implementation research is difficult for a variety of related reasons, including, for example:

- *There are no widely established or accepted technical standards for causal analysis in implementation research design.* Unlike impact evaluations, implementation studies do not have a well-established body of technical standards for designs aimed at probing for causal connections. In part, this is because the purposes of implementation research are so varied that there is no common analytic goal around which to formulate best research practices or approaches.

  Without a core body of accepted truths, implementation researchers cannot organize debates about which approach to use for what purpose and in what circumstances. Discussions about impact analysis almost always begin with the shared stipulation that the impact of program X is the difference between what happened under program X and what would have happened in the absence of X. The major area of debate is how best to measure "what would have happened in the absence of X." No such core concepts yet exist across all implementation research approaches and methods.

- *The approach used in implementation research sometimes rests on paradigms taken from different social science disciplines.* One of implementation research's great strengths—its eclecticism—may also be one of its great weaknesses. That is, its methods and orientations are often taken from different social science disciplines—such as political science, economics, psychology, anthropology, sociology, and demography—with different theoretical paradigms and different substantive domains.

- *The structure of explanations in implementation research often rests on underlying theories about how programs are developed, designed, and operated.* The very issue of where to look for causes explicitly or implicitly rests on a variety of theories about how programs work. For example, a Marxian social theorist may view social programs primarily as means for ruling groups to assert "social control" over marginal groups or groups whose interests are inimical to those in power (see Piven and Cloward 1990). In this context, implementation research becomes the study of how effectively programs and policies reinforce given power and status structures.

Less ideologically charged theories about program design and implementation also imply differing views of where to look for explanations of program operations or results.[2] For example, early practitioners of implementation research conceptualized program implementation as a hierarchical process of translating legislation and policy directives down through state and local agencies to individual program workers. In part, the idea of "street-level bureaucracy" (discussed in more detail below) was to turn the more traditional view on its head. In reality, according to the perspective of street-level bureaucracy, policy is actually determined at the time and place that frontline workers interact with the public. In many public agencies, such as those that provide cash assistance, frontline workers facing high levels of stress and too much demand for their time may develop coping mechanisms that determine how they deliver services and distribute benefits. Those coping mechanisms may not bear any direct relationship to official policy. To understand how and why policy gets implemented as it does, street-level bureaucracy argues, researchers must understand the incentives, constraints, and attitudes of the frontline staff and not necessarily the paths by which directives from above get translated along the hierarchical chain.

Despite the lack of consensus around core concepts in implementation research, many studies offer useful and cogent hypotheses about "why it is happening as it is." The remainder of this section reviews some of the approaches used to explain implementation.

Using the Program Model as a Provisional Theory of the Program

Just as the program model may be used as a reference point for *assessing* implementation, it is also used to help *explain* why a program is operating and performing as it is. As discussed in chapter 1, a program model is either implicitly or explicitly based on a theory or set of theories about causation and human behavior.[3] Within the context of a provisional acceptance of the theory implied in a program model, the model can provide a framework for understanding why programs do not operate as expected.

With this approach, when researchers observe variances from planned operations or expected results, they may refer to the program model or theory to determine which parts of the causal chain are missing or deviate from the model. Note that only variations need to be explained; if the program is operating as planned and if participants are behaving as expected, no explanation beyond the program theory is needed.[4] However, if all "parts" of the program model are in place and operating as planned, and the program still does not achieve it expected results, the program model may itself be called into question.

An example of the use of a program's model as a tool for explaining implementation problems comes from an evaluation of an early welfare reform demonstration in Alabama, the Alabama Avenues to Self-Sufficiency through Employment and Training Services (ASSETS) program (see Hargreaves et al. 1993; Werner et al. 1997). This demonstration program tested a variety of policy initiatives, including consolidating food stamps and AFDC into a single cash grant, simplifying and streamlining eligibility rules and procedures, and broadening the requirement for recipients to participate in employment and training services. One of the important goals of the program was to increase the employment and earnings of welfare clients and decrease their dependence on welfare benefits.

As part of the ASSETS program design, clients' employability assessment and referral to services was to be assisted by an automated administrative system. However, because the administrative system was not in place when ASSETS was first implemented, the employment and training requirement was administered selectively by case managers, and often not enforced. Partly as a result of ASSETS's streamlined eligibility process and because of the delay in implementing the automated administrative system, ASSETS actually increased welfare participation in the pilot counties without increasing clients' employment and earnings. Although the employment and training system was eventually "up and running," the use of these services never ramped up to intended scale over the course of the evaluation study. Because an integral part of the program model was not implemented as planned, ASSETS did not produce its hypothesized outcomes.

The evaluation of the GAIN program in California is an example of how implementation research may bring a program's model into question (see Riccio et al. 1994; Weissman 1997). GAIN was an ambitious approach to welfare reform that attempted to implement a comprehensive and continuous obligation for welfare recipients to engage in activities designed to lead to employment and financial independence. Although each county implementing GAIN had some flexibility in choosing which service stream to emphasize, the program's basic model called for an employability assessment dividing those needing upgrading in basic education skills from those not needing more basic education. Those needing education were usually given a choice of whether to engage first in a job search or enter an educational component. The demonstration counties adopted a variety of philosophies and administrative structures that heavily influenced these choices. Those counties emphasizing basic education for clients with poor educational attainment believed that such services would lead to better and more stable employment.

The six demonstration counties also made different decisions regarding which service paths to emphasize, resulting in a variety of participation patterns. As discussed earlier in this chapter, Riverside County was distinguished by its emphasis on a strong work attachment message and pervasive referral to early job search, even for those participants deemed in need of education. Most of the other study counties were more willing to allow those needing education to participate in basic education services before engaging in job service, on the theory (embodied by the program model) that such initial investments in human capital would ultimately pay off in better and more stable employment. Although the issue was not entirely clear-cut, the counties emphasizing early job search even for clients with low educational attainment generally had better employment results.[5] Dissatisfaction with clients' employment outcomes led Los Angeles County to abandon its emphasis on basic education services and to change the fundamental orientation of its GAIN program to a "work first" philosophy.

One version of this general framework for explaining program operations and results currently in vogue in evaluation research—the so-called "theory of change" approach—seemingly promises to produce conclusions about program impacts from descriptions of activities and observations of outcomes.[6] The analytic leverage of the approach arises from the deceptively simple principle that a social program's model either explicitly or implicitly embodies a set of predictions (or a "theory of the program") about how the program's interventions will change client behavior and circumstances. Once the program theory is laid out in detail, its predictions may be tested just like those of any scientific hypothesis. That is, if the specific interventions happen and lead to the predicted changes in client behavior and outcomes, the "program theory" is not falsified and so maintains its provisional credibility.

Although the theory of change approach conceptually links program design, operations, and outcomes, it also has limitations as a substitute for a more traditional impact design.[7] For example, it focuses intensively on participant experiences in program activities and services and the changes in participant outcomes following those experiences, but usually does not include observation of experiences outside of the program. Those outside experiences may influence and change participant outcomes. Moreover, even if the program has some effect on client outcomes, it may not be for the reasons expounded by the program theory.

The theory of change is particularly attractive when it is impossible or undesirable to implement a random assignment experiment. However, due to the problems discussed above and others, the most that can be hoped for in most applications of this approach is some judgment about the *feasibility* of the program's theory. That is, if the services are implemented as planned and the predicted changes in outcomes happen, it is *possible* that the program caused those changes. But to know that with certainty and to know how much of an impact the program caused almost always requires a research design that can estimate the counterfactual, or what those outcomes would have been in the absence of the program.

The Perspective of "Street-Level Bureaucracy"

Since its introduction as a fundamental orientation in understanding the workings of public institutions, street-level bureaucracy has made some important contributions to implementation research. By recognizing that frontline workers' incentives and motivations shape how policy is implemented, street-level bureaucracy helped focus attention on an otherwise neglected aspect of public administration. Its research orientation is particularly valuable during times of serious changes in policies and administrative culture, such as under welfare reform. It is particularly during those times that established routines and behaviors of frontline agency workers may be asked to change. According to the theory behind street-level bureaucracy, true policy is created out of the tension between the demands of new administrative rules and procedures and frontline workers' need to develop a new "comfort level" in doing their jobs. As a current practitioner of the street-level orientation in implementation research writes (Brodkin 2003, 145):

> This approach is most valuable when policy implementation involves change in organizational practice, discretion by frontline workers, and complex decision-making in a context of formal policy ambiguity and uncertainty. By focusing on specific institutions and the informal, lower-level routines through which they create policy at the point of delivery, it is possible to give greater transparency to policies that are otherwise opaque and provide a fuller picture of how policy is produced and experienced in everyday life.

The great appeal of the street-level perspective is that it focuses researchers' attention on what happens to official policy at the point of service delivery. But the approach also has some important limitations. For example, the basis for sometimes rather intricate conclusions about how and why worker discretion shapes policy implementation in a given program is often taken from the sketchy evidence of a few worker interviews and program observations. Occasionally, the street-level perspective and its interpretation seem to be used to confirm a researcher's biases and prior expectations about how a new policy or program will be received by frontline workers. It is not always clear how findings about what is really going on at the street level can be validated.

A second limitation lies in the practical value of the street-level perspective in shaping policy and program management. Although policymakers and program managers clearly have to take the reality of street-level bureaucracy into account, it is not an easy matter to devise ways of limiting worker discretion or of pushing that discretion in desired directions. Sometimes upper-level management concerns about too much worker discretion in the implementation of policy can lead to self-defeating administrative measures. For example, an excessive emphasis on automatic sanctions for program noncompliance could hamper caseworkers in their efforts to find the most effective way to move TANF families toward economic independence.

In a study of the implementation of mutual responsibility contracts, Evelyn Brodkin (1997) examines how worker discretion within the larger bureaucratic framework of a welfare agency determines how the state's end of the bargain with clients gets played out. Such contracts became more popular in the 1990s—and increasingly so after the creation of the TANF program—as formal mechanisms to make explicit both client work preparation responsibilities and agency service responsibilities.

Using the techniques of the street-level approach, Brodkin (1997) argues that the execution of the state's end of the bargain in the contract between client and welfare agency is fully dependent on frontline workers' decisions. Moreover, as frontline workers are the gatekeepers to benefits and services, clients cannot make alternative interpretations of the state's obligations under the contract. Caseworkers hold almost all the cards, and policymakers and agency managers must understand the caseworker perspective in order to implement policy effectively. But the caseworkers' perspective is shaped more by their immediate incentives, comfort level, training, experience, and command of resources, rather than by policy mandates or political ideology:

> Political rhetoric aside, neither policymakers in Washington nor managers in state agencies can presume to control what caseworkers believe or value. Nor in any real sense can they control what caseworkers do . . . by formulating more rules or imposing more production quotas . . . Caseworkers, like other lower-level bureaucrats, do not do just what they want or just what they are told to want. They do what they can. Their capacity depends on their professional skills, agency resources, and access to good training and employment opportunities for clients. Within that context, their practices are shaped by agency incentives and mechanisms that make staff accountable to clients and to the public (Brodkin 1997, 24).

Another example of how the perspective of street-level bureaucracy can illuminate implementation research is found in a study of the Work Pays Program in California (Meyers, Glaser, and MacDonald 1998). This study examined how caseworkers determine policy through the information and attitudes they communicate to clients. The major data collection effort was a structured observation of initial and ongoing eligibility interviews. These interviews noted in particular workers' implicit and explicit messages about how serious the agency was about the new work-oriented policies. The research found that workers failed to change their fundamental policy orientation and overwhelmingly fit the new rules into their more familiar and comfortable framework:

> In over 80 percent of intake and redetermination interviews workers did not provide and interpret information about welfare reforms. Most workers continued a pattern of instrumental transactions that emphasized workers' needs to collect and

verify eligibility information. Some workers coped with new demands by providing information about work-related policies, but routinizing the information and adding it to their standardized, scripted recitations of welfare rules. Others were coping by particularizing their interactions, giving some of their clients some information some of the time, on an ad hoc basis (Meyers et al. 1998, 18–19).

Statistical Approaches: Performance Analysis

Performance analysis—the statistical modeling of program outcomes as functions of administrative variables and other causal factors—goes further than other explanatory approaches to link the subject matter of implementation research with quantitative methods. Although some critics maintain that performance analysis is really impact analysis in another form, it does not pretend to estimate the overall impact of a program or of a set of policies. Rather, performance analysis has the potential to assess the impact of specific administrative arrangements and activities *within* a given programmatic and policy context and a given environment. In this sense, performance analysis has the potential to help maximize program outcomes.

Lawrence Mead (2003, 110), a leading practitioner of the approach, sets down its conceptual basis:

> The question is whether program units with measurable features . . . perform better on outcome indicators than those with different features, when one controls for differences in the clients and the labor market.

Some of the keys to sound performance analysis include choosing units of analysis (program units) that correspond roughly to areas of administrative discretion (such as supervisory units or local TANF offices); accurately describing the major discretionary features of those administrative units; and having enough variation in administrative approaches among the program units, and enough program units, to allow for adequate statistical precision. When researchers combine performance analysis with relevant control variables, such as measures of client employability and local economic and cultural factors, they can estimate the influence of administrative variables on program outcomes.

The characterization and measurement of administrative variables in performance analysis relies on many of the data collection and analysis techniques used in other implementation research approaches. Most notably, the method uses open-ended interviews and observations to identify office or worker styles and attitudes that may influence interactions with clients and, ultimately, client behavior. Moreover, the approach relies on similar methods to understand what a program's performance measurements—the "left-hand side" variables of the statistical models— actually present and whether they represent the same things across administrative units of analysis.

Mead (2003) also exposes some of the limitations of performance analysis. These include the following questions:

- Can administrative data really capture what happens in a program (e.g., what does an outcome of "completed job search" really mean)?
- Do administrative data elements mean the same thing across program units (e.g., does "completed job search" mean the same thing across individual workers or administrative units)?
- Are the explanatory variables used in performance analysis models really independent of one another or do they perhaps rely on higher-level structural factors or secular changes (e.g., overall state agency structure and philosophy or changing community views about welfare and working)?
- Can the method control for potential selection bias (e.g., bias introduced by workers choosing the most compliant clients on which to focus their efforts and/or by clients deciding to participate and/or take jobs in welfare-to-work programs)?

The foregoing issues notwithstanding, Mead and others have used performance analysis in an attempt to understand how various administrative arrangements and worker styles may influence client activities and outcomes. A particular focus of Mead's research has been the relationship of a program's administrative features to client participation and outcomes in welfare-to-work programs. A recent study by Carolyn J. Heinrich and Laurence Lynn (1999) of the relationship of the administrative and management structure of Job Training Partnership Act (JTPA) Service Delivery Areas (SDAs) and client outcomes is a good example of the approach.

Heinrich and Lynn (1999) used data from two levels of analytic units: (1) individual JTPA participants from 16 SDAs, and (2) the 16 SDAs that make decisions about JTPA programs, services, and governance. The individual-level data included demographic and employment history information, and the SDA-level data included information about administrative structures, performance incentive policies for service providers, service delivery and contracting strategies, and employment and labor market conditions. Because the individuals are nested in the 16 SDAs, the authors used hierarchical linear modeling (HLM).

The study found positive relationships between several management and administrative strategies and participant outcomes. For example, it found a large, positive, and significant impact on post-program earnings when the administrative entity directing the SDA was a private industry council (PIC), as opposed to a local elected official or the CEO of a private, for-profit firm. The study also confirmed that policies that strengthen performance incentives have positive impacts on participant post-program earnings. The study also found that SDAs that contract out for more services perform better than those that provide services directly. Assuming that the statistics are sound and that the administrative and management variables are accurate and valid measures of what really happens in practice, this study demonstrates the potential of the performance measurement approach in yielding results that may be directly useful to program designers and managers.

Ethnographic Approaches

Ethnographic approaches were introduced in this book as strategies for descriptive analysis. But ethnography also has promise as an explanatory approach in implementation research. By allowing a window into how program policies, operations, services, and benefits fit into the rich texture of clients' lives,

> ethnographic research . . . can flesh out the ecological context (a kin network, a neighborhood, a transportation system, a legal system, a local labor market) of the clients' lives, and can reveal how various aspects of that context may encourage or interfere with client responses to the program or policy (Edin 2003, 168).

Typical criticisms of the use of ethnography in research designed to inform policy choices are similar to those usually aimed at many forms of nonstatistical (qualitative) analysis. For example, regardless of the unit of analysis (e.g., individuals, families, welfare offices, neighborhoods) ethnographic research rarely adopts a scientific sampling strategy. Ethnographic analyses are taken to be "anecdotal," with their external validity in question. Moreover, the measures and constructs used in ethnographic research are rarely specified with the precision and uniformity required by statistical analysis. Finally, the fundamental orientation of ethnography is often exploratory, with researchers coming to the subject matter with a "blank slate" rather than with testable hypotheses.

While well taken, these common criticisms may miss the major point of using ethnographic research in implementation studies. Ethnography's power to illuminate comes in large part from the ethnographer's suspension of preconceived notions about how clients and workers perceive and interact with policies and programs. In this way, ethnography has the potential to view program implementation in a fresh light and to refine measures and constructs used in statistical analysis, help frame hypotheses to be tested with more rigorous designs, or to add insight into the causal chain linking policies and programs with client outcomes.

The latter points are well illustrated by the study "Making Ends Meet: How Single Mothers Survive Welfare and Low-Wage Work," by Kathryn Edin and Laura Lein (1997). The study developed out of a survey of low-income single mothers in which nearly half of the families in poverty reported expenses that outstripped their incomes. To get behind these numbers and understand them (or debunk them), the authors found that they had to abandon traditional survey research methods and adopt an ethnographic approach to the subject matter. That is, they had to approach the women in the study without preconceived notions about which questions to ask, how to ask them, and what the responses really meant. Moreover, the authors found that they had to develop trust with their respondents in order to probe sensitive topics and expect honest and complete answers.

Adopting an ethnographic approach in the Edin and Lein study helped the researchers to confirm the earlier survey's finding that many welfare-dependent low-income families do have expenses that exceed their benefits from multiple programs, or from the combination of those benefits and reported earnings. They found that many of the mothers in these families worked steadily or from time to time in unreported jobs and/or at illegal pursuits to make ends meet. The authors conclude that an adequate welfare reform strategy to replace assistance entirely with earnings would have to place single mothers in relatively well-paying jobs, with wages about twice the minimum wage. Their conclusions are complemented by impact studies of welfare reform programs and studies of TANF leavers that find that many families leaving welfare for work do not escape poverty.

Concluding Remarks

This chapter surveyed a range of strategies available to implementation researchers when assessing or explaining implementation. These aspects of implementation research in particular can be most useful to policymakers and program operators serving the public interest in designing, developing, managing, and improving social programs.

Reliable and useful assessment and explanation in implementation research rest first of all on adequate and accurate data collection and program description. If the basic facts about a program are wrong or incomplete, it is easy to make incorrect judgments in assessing a program's success or in explaining its operations and results. This chapter argues, however, that even given accurate and well-organized descriptive data, assessing or explaining implementation requires some careful choices.

When assessing implementation, the major choice is among the available models, norms, or standards against which to rate program operations and results. Because program assessments are relative, they can turn on the choice of comparative standards. That choice is open to question and should be made clear and defensible by researchers on the basis of its objectivity, fairness, and usefulness. It may be argued that the fairest standards are those set by program plans and expectations, and that programs should only be judged on their own terms. On the other hand, implementation researchers may sometimes wish to consider other perspectives, such as overall social welfare or social values.

In explaining implementation, researchers develop hypotheses about why programs work as they do. Such hypotheses may be useful in improving program operations and results and in guiding future program realizations. As when assessing implementation, researchers make implicit or explicit choices. Their choices are not concerned with standards, but rather with the overall causal framework in which to understand how programs work.

The framework used to explain implementation may be *internal* to the program and rest on the provisional theory or theories motivating program design. Alternatively, the causal framework may be *external* to the program and rest on grander theories about how forces in society at large, or within the bureaucracy itself, interact to shape program experiences and outcomes. Finally, the causal framework may rest on an intimate understanding of how the program fits into program stakeholders' lives and activities. As with the choices made in assessing implementation, those made in explaining implementation should be clear and defensible. At a minimum, an explanation of program implementation should generate testable hypotheses.

NOTES

1. When the JOBS Program was created, the American Public Welfare Association (APWA; now, the American Public Human Services Association—APHSA) developed materials intended to identify and make recommendations about best practices for JOBS caseworkers.

2. For more background on the recent history of theories of program implementation, see Kaplan and Corbett (2003).

3. This is the fundamental insight of the theory of change approach to program evaluation. A problematic issue for the theory of change is whether it provides an adequate structure for assessing impacts in the absence of some additional design to measure the counterfactual. That is, although each implementation of a program is certainly an *implicit* test of its theoretical foundations, and, although exposing those foundations is desirable, some acceptable design must be imposed in order to make the specific implementation an *explicit* test of the theory.

4. Of course, such a program experience does not "prove" the program's theory. It only fails to disprove it.

5. Note that the implementation research studies for ASSETS and for GAIN were done within the context of a comprehensive evaluation that included impact and cost-benefit studies.

6. Joseph Wholey and Carol Weiss were among the initial developers and major popularizers of the theory of change approach to program evaluation. See, for example, Weiss (1997b).

7. Many of the apparent shortcomings of the theory of change approach are exposed and discussed by Weiss (1997a).

References

Abt Associates, Inc. 2001. "Civic Engagement through Community Service: Assessment of Long-Term Impacts on Service Participants." Cambridge: Abt Associates Inc.

Acs, Gregory, and Pamela Loprest. 2001a. "Initial Synthesis Report of the Findings from ASPE's 'Leavers' Grants." Washington, DC: The Urban Institute.

———. 2001b. "The Status of TANF Leavers in the District of Columbia: Final Report." Washington, DC: The Urban Institute.

American Public Human Services Association. 1993. *JOBS Case Management Handbook.* Washington, DC: American Public Human Services Association.

———. 1994. *Managing JOBS Caseloads.* Washington, DC: American Public Human Services Association.

Atkinson, Paul, and Martyn Hammersley. 1994. "Ethnography and Participant Observation." In *Handbook of Qualitative Research,* edited by Norman K. Denzin and Yvonna S. Lincoln (236–47). Thousand Oaks, CA: Sage Publications.

Bloom, Dan, and David Butler. 1995. *Implementing Time-Limited Welfare: Early Experiences in Three States.* New York: Manpower Demonstration Research Corporation.

Bloom, Dan, Mary Farell, James J. Kemple, and Nandita Verma. 1999. *The Family Transition Program: Implementation and Three-Year Impacts of Florida's Initial Time-Limited Welfare Program.* New York: Manpower Demonstration Research Corporation.

Brodkin, Evelyn. 1997. "Inside the Welfare Contract: Discretion and Accountability in State Welfare Administration." *Social Service Review* 71(1): 1–33.

———. 2003. "Street-Level Research: Policy at the Front Lines." In *Policy into Action: Implementation Research and Welfare Reform,* edited by Mary Clare Lennon and Thomas Corbett (145–64). Washington, DC: Urban Institute Press.

Charlesworth, Leanne, and Catherine Born. 2003. "Approaches to Data Collection." In *Policy into Action: Implementation Research and Welfare Reform,* edited by Mary Clare Lennon and Thomas Corbett (239–80). Washington, DC: Urban Institute Press.

Corbett, Thomas. 1997. "Getting Inside the 'Black Box' in an Era of Policy Discontinuity: Doing Good Process Evaluations." Unpublished manuscript. Madison: University of Wisconsin.

Dean, Debra L. 1994. "How to Use Focus Groups." In *Handbook of Practical Program Evaluation,* edited by Joseph S. Whaley, Harry P. Hatry, and Kathryn E. Newcomer (338–49). San Francisco: Jossey-Boss Publishers.

Edin, Kathryn, and Laura Lein. 1997. *Making Ends Meet: How Single Mothers Survive Welfare and Low-Wage Work.* New York: Russell Sage Foundation.

———. 2003. "Client-Based Ethnographic Research as a Tool for Implementation Analysis." In *Policy into Action: Implementation Research and Welfare Reform,* edited by Mary Clare Lennon and Thomas Corbett (165–92). Washington, DC: Urban Institute Press.

Fowler, Jr., Floyd J. 1984. *Survey Research Methods.* Beverly Hills, CA: Sage Publications.

Frees, J. W., and Meryl Finkel. 1991. "Final Report of the Evaluation of the Model Employment and Training Program." Cambridge: Abt Associates Inc.

Gordon, Anne, Carole Kuhns, Renee Loeffler, and Roberto Agodini. 1999. *Experiences of Virginia Time Limit Families in the Six Months after Case Closure: Results for an Early Cohort.* Princeton: Mathematica Policy Research.

Hagen, Jan L., and Irene Lurie. 1992. "Implementing JOBS: Initial State Choices." Albany: The Nelson A. Rockefeller College of Public Affairs and Policy.

———. 1993. "Implementing JOBS: The Initial Design and Structure of Local Programs." Albany: The Nelson A. Rockefeller College of Public Affairs and Policy.

———. 1994a. "Implementing JOBS: The Participants' Perspective." Albany: The Nelson A. Rockefeller College of Public Affairs and Policy.

———. 1994b. "Implementing JOBS: Progress and Promise." Albany: State University of New York.

Hargreaves, Margaret, Alan Werner, and Pamela Joshi. 1995. "The Evaluation of To Strengthen Michigan Families: Process Report." Cambridge: Abt Associates Inc.

Hargreaves, Margaret, Alan Werner, Steven Mennemeyer, and Gayle Wykle. 1993. "Evaluation of the Alabama Avenues to Self-Sufficiency through Employment and Training Services (ASSETS) Demonstration: Interim Implementation and Process Report." Cambridge, MA: Abt Associates.

Heinrich, Carolyn J., and Laurence E. Lynn, Jr. 1999. "Governance and Performance: The Influence of Program Structure and Management on Job Training Partnership (JTPA) Program Outcomes." Working Paper. Chicago: The Irving B. Harris School of Public Policy Studies, University of Chicago.

Kaplan, Thomas, and Thomas Corbett. 2003. "Three Generations of Implementation Research: Looking for the Keys to Implementation 'Success.'" In *Policy into Action: Implementation Research and Welfare Reform,* edited by Mary Clare Lennon and Thomas Corbett (57–71). Washington, DC: Urban Institute Press.

Krueger, Richard A. 1988. *Focus Groups: A Practical Guide for Applied Research.* Newbury Park, CA: Sage Publications.

Kuhn, Thomas. 1962. *The Structure of Scientific Revolution.* Chicago: Chicago University Press.

Lennon, Mary Clare, and Thomas Corbett, editors. 2003. *Policy into Action: Implementation Research and Welfare Reform.* Washington, DC: Urban Institute Press.

Lipsky, Michael. 1980. *Street-Level Bureaucracy: The Dilemmas of Individuals in Social Services.* Cambridge, MA: MIT Press.

Mead, Lawrence. 2003. "Performance Analysis." In *Policy into Action: Implementation Research and Welfare Reform,* edited by Mary Clare Lennon and Thomas Corbett (107–144). Washington, DC: Urban Institute Press.

Meyers, Marcia K., Bonnie Glaser, and Karin MacDonald. 1998. "On the Front Lines of Welfare Delivery: Are Workers Implementing Policy Reforms?" *Journal of Policy Analysis and Management* 17(1): 1–22.

Miles, Matthew B., and A. Michael Huberman. 1984. *Qualitative Data Analysis.* Beverly Hills: Sage Publishing.

Miller, Thomas. 1994. "Designing and Conducting Surveys." In *Handbook of Practical Program Evaluation,* edited by Joseph S. Whaley, Harry P. Hatry, and Kathryn E. Newcomer (271–92). San Francisco: Jossey-Boss Publishers.

Nightingale, Demetra Smith, and Shelli Balter Rossman. 1994. "Managing Field Data Collection from Start to Finish." In *Handbook of Practical Program Evaluation,* edited by Joseph S. Wholey, Harry P. Hatry, and Kathryn E. Newcomer (350–73). San Francisco: Jossey-Bass.

Piven, Franes Fox, and Richard D. Cloward. 1990. *Regulating the Poor: The Functions of Public Welfare.* New York: Vintage Books.

Riccio, James, and Yeheskel Hasenfeld. 1996. "Enforcing a Participation Mandate in a Welfare-to-Work Program." *Social Service Review* 70(4): 516–42.

Riccio, James, Daniel Friedlander, and Stephen Freedman. 1994. *GAIN: Benefits, Costs, and Three-Year Impacts of a Welfare-to-Work Program.* New York: Manpower Demonstration Research Corporation.

Scrivener, Susan, Gayle Hamilton, Mary Farrell, Stephen Freedman, Daniel Friedlander, Marisa Mitchell, Jodi Nudelman, and Christine Schwartz. 1998. "National Evaluation of Welfare-to-Work Strategies: Implementation, Participation Patterns, Costs, and Two-Year Impacts of the Portland (Oregon) Welfare-to-Work Program." New York: Manpower Demonstration Research Corporation.

St. Pierre, Robert, Anne Ricciuti, Fumiyo Tao, and Cindy Creps. 2000. "Third National Even Start Evaluation: Interim Report." Cambridge: Abt Associates, Inc.

Weiss, Carol. 1997a. "How Can Theory-Based Evaluation Make Greater Headway?" *Evaluation Review* 21(4): 501–24.

———. 1997b. "Theory-Based Evaluation: Past, Present, and Future." In *Progress and Future Directions in Evaluation: Perspectives on Theory, Practice, and Methods,* edited by D. J. Rog and D. Fournier. San Francisco: Jossey-Bass.

Weissman, Evan. 1997. "Changing to a Work First Strategy: Lessons from Los Angeles County's GAIN Program for Welfare Recipients." New York: Manpower Demonstration Research Corporation.

Werner, Alan, and Bonnie Nutt-Powell. 1988. *Evaluation of the Implementation of the New York State Comprehensive Employment Opportunity Support Centers: Volume I— Synthesis of Findings.* Cambridge: Abt Associates, Inc.

Werner, Alan, David Rodda, Elsie Pan, and Lisa Plimpton. 1997. "Evaluation of the Alabama Avenues to Self-Sufficiency through Employment and Training Services (ASSETS) Demonstration: Final Report." Cambridge, MA: Abt Associates.

Wolcott, Harry F. 1994. *Transforming Qualitative Data: Description, Analysis, and Interpretation.* Thousand Oaks: Sage Publishing.

About the Author

Alan Werner is a principal associate at Abt Associates, Inc., where for the past 18 years he has designed and conducted numerous large-scale comprehensive evaluations for state and federal agencies. His principal policy areas are welfare reform and employment policy for low-income workers. Before coming to Abt Associates, Dr. Werner was the director of research for the Massachusetts Department of Public Welfare. He has also conducted research and taught courses in the history of social welfare policy and in ethics and public policy at the Florence Heller School for Advanced Studies in Social Welfare at Brandeis University.

Index

administrative data, 29–33, 54
  automated, 58–59
  collecting hard-copy, 54, 56, 58
  hard-copy *vs.* automated administrative files, 30–32
administrative modeling, 25n.6
agencies, responsible
  resources and capacity to implement program, 3–4
Alabama Avenues to Self-Sufficiency through Employment and Training Services (ASSETS), 136–137
assessing implementation, 7, 9, 119–122, 145–146
  standards for
    broader social standards, 120, 126, 128–129
    client perspectives, 132. *See also* client assessment of program services
    federal participation standards, 120, 126–128
    industry or exemplary programs, 120–121, 129–131
    legislatively mandated standards, 126–128
    professional experience and judgment, 121, 131

    program model, plan, or design, 120, 122–125
    rules specifying program content and performance standards, 120, 126
    stakeholder opinions and judgment, 121, 131–132
    worker perspectives, 132, 133
automated administrative data, 31, 58–59
  approaches to collecting, 58
automated systems, 31, 84–85
automated *vs.* hard-copy administrative files, 30–32
Avenues to Self-Sufficiency through Employment and Training Services (ASSETS), 136–137

Brodkin, Evelyn, 139–140

child care programs, subsidized, 84–85
children's school activity after leaving welfare, 106
client assessment of program services, 107, 109, 132
client characteristics, 94–97
client flow, 88

client flow model, 89, 91
client outcomes, 104–105. *See also*
    outcomes
    changes in, 105–106
client satisfaction surveys, 64, 66–67, 107,
    109
client surveys, 63–64. *See also* surveys
client understanding of program policies,
    107, 108
Comprehensive Employment Opportu-
    nity Support Center (CEOSC),
    21–22, 125
confidentiality, 53
contextual information, providing, 10
cost-effectiveness, 11
cross-sectional analyses, 98

data, 6–7
    accuracy/reliability, 36–37
        maximizing, 37–38
        reasons for inaccuracies, 37
    across researchers, synthesizing, 86–87
    comparability, 39–40
    representativeness (external validity),
        38–39
data collection, 6–7. *See also specific topics*
    cost, 40–41
    and data sources, depth *vs.* breadth of,
        40–42
    on-site, 48, 50–54
data collection activities, 54. *See also spe-
    cific topics*
data collection strategies
    considerations in, 36–40
    and data sources, linking research
        questions with, 74–77
data needs and sources, 27–28
    administrative data, 29–33
    observations of program activities and
        services, 35
    oral accounts, descriptions, opinions,
        and recommendations, 33–34
    purposes, 33–34
    printed material, 28–29
    survey and program questionnaire
        data, 35–36
documenting implementation, 7, 8, 81
documents needed for implementation
    studies, 28–29

Edin, Kathryn, 113, 114, 143
employment and training program, 104
EMPOWER program, 109, 111
environment, program, 75, 115
    suitability of program to, 16, 23
ethnographic approaches to explaining
    implementation, 143–144
ethnographic data
    providing, 10
    used to develop hypotheses, 113, 114
ethnographic research and data collec-
    tion, 73, 112–113
    types of, 73–74
ethnography, 73
evaluation. *See* assessing implementation
Even Start Family Literacy Program, 126
explaining implementation, 7, 9,
    133–135, 145–146
    ethnographic approaches, 143–144
    perspective of "street-level bureau-
        cracy," 138–141
    statistical approaches, 141–143
    using program model as provisional
        theory of program, 135–138
exploratory tools, 59

Family Transition Program (FTP), 96,
    103
federal participation standards, 120,
    126–128
feedback, providing rapid, 10
field visits. *See also* interviews
    post-visit activities, 48
    preparing for, 45
        establishing on-site contact person,
            46
        gaining clearance and informing
            sites, 45–46
        sending materials in advance of site
            visit, 46–47
fieldwork training manual, 48, 49
flexibility of implementation research
    agenda, 21–22
focus group guide, 61, 62
focus groups, 6, 59–60, 108–109, 111, 112
    designing, 60–61

Glaser, Bonnie, 140–141

graphic presentations, using, 89–92
Greater Avenues for Independence
        (GAIN), 130–131, 137

implementation research
    advantages, 10–11
    defined, 5, 24n.1
    illustrative questions, 1–5, 14–23
    limitations, 11–12
    nature of, 1–5
    purpose, 2, 81
    reasons for engaging in, 24–25n.4
    research methods included in, 5
        data and data collection, 6–7
        types of analyses used, 7–9
implementation research questions and
        descriptive analysis strategies,
        113, 115–116
interviews. See also under stakeholder
        perspectives
    conducting, 51–53
    for the field, designing, 44–45
    on-site
        conducting, 41
        planning, 43–48
        which respondents to interview, 43
    open-ended, 6, 38, 52, 53
        developing instruments for, 38,
            50–52
        synthesizing responses to, 83–85

Job Opportunity and Basic Skills (JOBS),
        92, 99–102, 117n.7
Job Training Partnership Act (JTPA), 142

"leavers studies" (welfare reform),
        105–106, 128–129
Lein, Laura, 113, 114
longitudinal analyses, 98

MacDonald, Karin, 140–141
Mead, Lawrence, 141, 142
Meyers, Marcia K., 140–141

observation guide for intake and redeter-
        mination sessions, 54, 55

observations, on-site
    conducting, 41, 53–55
    how many and which "units" to
        observe, 43–44
    planning/designing, 43–48, 53–55
    of program activities and services, 35
    which activities to observe, 43
on-site contact person, establishing, 46
outcomes, 5, 20–21, 23, 24n.3, 77, 116.
        See also client outcomes
    vs. impacts, 24n.3
    at "micro" and "macro" level, 20

participant observation, 6
performance analysis, 141–143
    conceptual basis, 141
    defined, 141
    limitations, 142
performance standards. See assessing
        implementation, standards for
Personal Responsibility and Work
        Opportunity Reconciliation Act
        (PRWORA), 13
policies. See program policies
population vs. sample, 94
pre-employment training (PET), 104
process studies, 17
professional assessment of implementa-
        tion. See under assessing imple-
        mentation, standards for
program design, 2–3. See also under
        assessing implementation, stan-
        dards for
program exit decisions, surveys about, 64,
        65
program managers, rapid feedback pro-
        vided to, 10
program narrative, 116n.1
    ordering, 88–89
    organizing data for, 82–83
        combining multiple accounts, 83–85
        synthesizing data across researchers,
            86–87
    preparing, 87
        level of detail, 87–88
program policies
    client understanding of, 107, 108
    staff acceptance and assessment of,
        107, 110

program processes and systems, operation of, 17–19, 23, 76, 115
program status, clients'
change in, over time, 101–102
program(s)
"as it really is," information provided about, 11
formative period of, information provided during, 10
goals and requirements, 2, 15
impacts, 11
theoretical and practical basis, 22, 75, 115

qualitative vs. quantitative data, 11, 116n.1
questions. See also interviews; surveys
guidelines for obtaining accurate answers to, 38
reviewing responses for consistency, 83

representativeness of data, 38–39
resource requirements and capacity, 22, 76
resources
needed to implement program, 3–4, 16
needed to operate program, 17, 115
Riverside Greater Avenues for Independence (GAIN), 130–131, 137

sample size, 70–71
vs. "depth" of data, 40–42
"sample" vs. "universe," 94
Service Delivery Areas (SDAs), 142–143
social practices and norms. See ethnographic research
social standards. See under assessing implementation, standards for
staff acceptance and assessment of program policies and services, 107, 110
staff training and preparation, 47–48
stakeholder opinions and judgment, 121, 131–132
stakeholder perspectives, reporting, 106–107

focus groups, 108–109, 111, 112
in-depth interviews and ethnographic research, 112–113
survey data, 107–110
statistics, 141–143
comparative, 97
descriptive, 92–94, 116n.1
client characteristics, 94–97
client outcomes, 104–106
program experiences and participation patterns, 98–104
"street-level bureaucracy" perspective, 138–141
subjective vs. objective data, 11
survey modes, 72–73
survey questionnaire data, 35–36. See also under stakeholder perspectives
survey samples. See also sample size
levels of precision for, 70–71
survey sampling, 70–71
surveys, 61, 63
about program exit decisions, 64, 65
client satisfaction, 64, 66–67, 107, 109
content, 63–64
designing, 64, 69–70
response rates and nonresponse bias, 72
types of, 63

tables used to present variations across research sites, 89, 92
variation in program content by state, 92, 93
variation in program features by state, 92
target population
reaching, with appropriate services, 5, 19–20, 23, 77, 116
Temporary Assistance for Needy Families (TANF), 50, 61, 98. See also specific topics
automated administrative systems and data, 31, 58
client participation in work-related activities
incidence of, 99, 100
length of, 99, 100
form used in application process, 56, 57

informing sites and gaining clearance for site visits, 45–46
interview guide for TANF case manager, 52
lack of industry standards in TANF programs, 129–130
"leavers studies," 105–106, 128–129
PRWORA and, 13
survey about program exit decisions, 64, 65
theory of change approach, 137–138
To Strengthen Michigan Families (TSMF), 107, 110, 132, 133

validity, external, 38–39

welfare agency worker survey, 64, 68
welfare programs, paradigm change in design of, 13–14
welfare reform, challenges of, 12–14
welfare reform program(s), 68, 102, 103, 109, 111. See also Temporary Assistance for Needy Families
research questions in designing study of a, 14–21
welfare-to-work strategies, 100, 132
Work First program, 60–61, 131
Work Pays Program, 140–141
worker assessment of implementation, 132, 133
worker surveys, 64. See also surveys